Watir Recipes

The problem solving guide to Watir

Zhimin Zhan

Watir Recipes

The problem solving guide to Watir

Zhimin Zhan

ISBN 978-1-50-588395-4

Leanpub

This is a Leanpub book. Leanpub empowers authors and publishers with the Lean Publishing process. Lean Publishing is the act of publishing an in-progress ebook using lightweight tools and many iterations to get reader feedback, pivot until you have the right book and build traction once you do.

Also By Zhimin Zhan

Selenium WebDriver Recipes in Ruby

Selenium WebDriver Recipes in Java

Learn Ruby Programming by Examples

Learn Swift Programming by Examples

Selenium WebDriver Recipes in Python

API Testing Recipes in Ruby

Selenium WebDriver Recipes in Node.js

Practical Continuous Testing

To Xindi, for your understanding and support. Thank you!

Contents

Preface   i
Who should read this book   ii
How to read this book   ii
Get recipe test scripts   ii
Send me feedback   iii

1. Introduction   1
   1.1   Watir and its variants   1
   1.2   RSpec   2
   1.3   Run recipe scripts   3

2. Watir and Selenium WebDriver   9
   2.1   Install Selenium Browser Drivers   9
   2.2   Cross browser testing with Watir   10
   2.3   Selenium WebDriver Locators   11
   2.4   Locating elements in Watir   11
   2.5   Access underneath Selenium API   12

3. Hyperlink   15
   3.1   Start browser   15
   3.2   Click a link by text   15
   3.3   Click Nth link with the same link text   17
   3.4   Verify a link present or not?   18
   3.5   Getting link data attributes   18
   3.6   Test links open a new browser window   19

4. Button   21
   4.1   Click a button by text   21
   4.2   Click a button by ID   22
   4.3   Click a button by name   22

4.4	Click an image button	. . . .	22
4.5	Assert a button present	. . . .	22
4.6	Assert a button displayed or hidden?	. . . .	23
4.7	Assert a button enabled or disabled?	. . . .	23

5. TextField and TextArea **25**

5.1	Enter text into a text field by name	. . . .	25
5.2	Enter text into a text field by ID	. . . .	25
5.3	Enter text into a password field	. . . .	26
5.4	Clear a text field	. . . .	26
5.5	Enter text into a multi-line text area	. . . .	26
5.6	Assert value	. . . .	26
5.7	Focus on a control	. . . .	27
5.8	Set a value to a read-only or disabled text field	. . . .	27

6. Radio button **29**

6.1	Select radio button by name and value	. . . .	29
6.2	Select radio button by ID	. . . .	29
6.3	Clear radio option selection	. . . .	29
6.4	Assert a radio option is selected	. . . .	30
6.5	Iterate radio buttons in a radio group	. . . .	30

7. CheckBox **31**

7.1	Select by name	. . . .	31
7.2	Select by ID	. . . .	31
7.3	Uncheck a checkbox	. . . .	31
7.4	Assert a checkbox is checked (or not)	. . . .	32

8. Select List **33**

8.1	Select an option by text or value	. . . .	33
8.2	Select an option by ID	. . . .	34
8.3	Select an option by iterating all options	. . . .	34
8.4	Select multiple options	. . . .	34
8.5	Clear selection	. . . .	35
8.6	Assert selected option	. . . .	35
8.7	Assert the value of a select list	. . . .	35
8.8	Assert option text in a select list	. . . .	36
8.9	Assert multiple selections	. . . .	36

9. **Navigation and Browser** 37
    9.1   Go to a URL 37
    9.2   Go to pages within the site without specifying full URL 37
    9.3   Perform actions from right click context menu such as 'Back', 'Forward' or
           'Refresh' 38
    9.4   Maximize browser window 38
    9.5   Minimize browser window 38
    9.6   Set typing speed 39
    9.7   Attaching browser 40
    9.8   Reuse browser 40
    9.9   Resizing browser window 41
    9.10   Remember current web page URL, then come back to it later 42
    9.11   Scroll to the bottom of a page 42
    9.12   Scroll to focus on a control 43
    9.13   Switch browser or tab 43

10. **Assertion** 45
    10.1   Assert page title 45
    10.2   Assert page text 45
    10.3   Assert page source 46
    10.4   Assert browser status 46
    10.5   Assert label text 47
    10.6   Assert span text 47
    10.7   Assert div text or HTML 47
    10.8   Assert table text 48
    10.9   Assert text in a table cell 49
    10.10 Assert text in a table row 49
    10.11 Assert image present 49

11. **Frames** 51
    11.1   Testing Frames 51
    11.2   Testing iframe 52
    11.3   Test multiple iframes 53

12. **Testing AJAX** 55
    12.1   Wait within a time frame 55
    12.2   Explicit Waits until Time out 56
    12.3   Implicit Waits until Time out 57
    12.4   Wait an object to be present 58

13. File Upload and Popup dialogs **59**

13.1   File upload 59

13.2   JavaScript pop ups 60

13.3   Timeout on an operation 61

13.4   Popup Handler approach 61

13.5   Handle JavaScript dialog with Popup Handler 62

13.6   Basic or Proxy Authentication dialog 63

13.7   Internet Explorer modal dialog 63

14. Debugging Test Scripts **65**

14.1   Print text for debugging 65

14.2   Write text to IDE output 65

14.3   Write page source or element HTML into a file 66

14.4   Take screenshot 66

14.5   Using IRB 67

14.6   Leave browser open after test finishes 67

14.7   Pause/Stop test execution at a certain step 68

14.8   Run selected test steps against current browser 69

15. Test Data **71**

15.1   Get date dynamically 71

15.2   Get a random boolean value 72

15.3   Generate a number within a range 72

15.4   Get a random character 73

15.5   Get a random string at fixed length 73

15.6   Get a random string in a collection 73

15.7   Generate random person names, emails, addresses with Faker 73

15.8   Generate a test file at fixed sizes 74

15.9   Retrieve data from Database 74

16. Browser Profile and Capabilities **77**

16.1   Get browser type and version 77

16.2   Set HTTP Proxy for Browser 77

16.3   Verify file download in Chrome 78

16.4   Test downloading PDF in Firefox 78

16.5   Start Firefox with extension 79

16.6   Manage Cookies 79

16.7   Headless Chrome 80

16.8   Test responsive websites 81

17. Advanced User Interactions **83**

   17.1   Double click a control 83

   17.2   Move mouse to a control - Mouse Over 84

   17.3   Click and hold - select multiple items 84

   17.4   Context Click - right click a control 85

   17.5   Drag and drop 85

   17.6   Drag slider 86

   17.7   Send key sequences - Select All and Delete 87

18. HTML 5 and JavaScript **89**

   18.1   HTML5 Email type field 89

   18.2   HTML5 Time Field 89

   18.3   Invoke 'onclick' JavaScript event 91

   18.4   Invoke JavaScript events such as 'onchange' 92

   18.5   Chosen - Standard Select 92

   18.6   Chosen - Multiple Select 94

   18.7   AngularJS web pages 97

   18.8   Ember JS web pages 100

   18.9   "Share Location" with Firefox 101

   18.10 Faking Geolocation with JavaScript 102

19. WYSIWYG HTML editors **103**

   19.1   TinyMCE 103

   19.2   CKEditor 104

   19.3   SummerNote 105

   19.4   CodeMirror 106

20. Leverage Programming **109**

   20.1   Raise exceptions to fail test 109

   20.2   Read external file 111

   20.3   Data-Driven Tests with Excel 112

   20.4   Data-Driven Tests with CSV 113

   20.5   Identify element IDs with dynamically generated long prefixes 113

   20.6   Sending special keys such as Enter to an element or browser 114

   20.7   Use of Unicode in test scripts 115

   20.8   Extract a group of dynamic data : verify search results in order 115

   20.9   Verify uniqueness of a set of data 116

   20.10 Extract dynamic visible data rows from a results table 116

   20.11 Extract dynamic text following a pattern using Regex 118

20.12 Quick extract pattern text in comments with Regex 119

20.13 Invoke element's JavaScript events such as 'onclick' 120

21. Optimization **123**

21.1 Assert text in page_source is faster than the text 123

21.2 Getting text from more specific element is faster 124

21.3 Avoid programming if-else block code if possible 124

21.4 Use variable to cache not-changed data 125

21.5 Enter large text into a text box 126

21.6 Use Environment Variables to change test behaviours dynamically 126

21.7 Test web site in two languages 127

21.8 Multi-language testing with lookups 129

22. Gotchas **131**

22.1 Test starts browser but no execution with blank screen 131

22.2 Failed to assert copied text in browser 132

22.3 The same test works for Chrome, but not IE 133

22.4 Element is not clickable or not visible 134

22.5 Lack knowledge of the programming language 134

23. Watir with Cucumber **135**

23.1 How Watir is integrated with Cucumber? 136

23.2 Execute Cucumber tests 137

23.3 Cucumber or RSpec? 139

Afterword **141**

Resources **143**

Books 143

Websites 144

Tools 144

Preface

In 2011, I presented at an international conference on software testing. I was really impressed with tester's desire to embrace automate test web applications. The audience surrounded me with various questions after my sessions. The following year, I was invited to present at the same conference. The enthusiastic atmosphere was the same, if not stronger ('Test Automation' and 'Web application testing' were listed as No.1 and No.2 of top 10 hot topics in the audience survey). I did recognize a couple of familiar faces. When I asked them casually how their test automation was going in their projects. They either said "not so good" or shied away. This got me thinking on my trip back.

Not long after, I was coaching test automation on a client site. The only tester there was completely new to test automation, but she was quite keen to learn. At the end of the day, she did well, developed a dozen of automated test cases. I then asked her: "After you read my book or attended one of my presentations, would you go back to try test automation in your project". "No", she quickly answered, "I would believe in it, but I will not have the confidence to give it a try at work." Suddenly, I knew why some of my audience were so keen on test automation but dared not put it into practice at work: lack of confidence.

Everyone in the field understands that manual testing is the bottleneck of software development and performing regression testing is practically impossible for many projects. As a result, long release cycles and poor quality products. Few testers consider manual testing exciting and fun (I can tell you that test automation is). Motivated managers or testers want to change that. However, the knowledge they gain from books or presentations would not give them enough confidence and courage to take action.

Therefore, test automation is rarely done successfully. From executive's perspective, they usually are more cautious after having seen several failed attempts on test automation. Practically, for motivated project managers or test team leaders who plan to introduce test automation, they need to have a secret trial. They usually develop some simple tests by following the start guide. However, they will soon face some challenges such as: clicking this dynamic generated hyperlink, handling base authentication pop ups, ..., etc. Often, they got stuck there.

The motivation for me to write this book: to guide these motivated test professionals with writing test scripts in Watir, a popular Ruby testing library for automating web browsers.

This book contains over 160 recipes for testing web applications with Watir. If you have read my other book 'Practical Web Test Automation[1]', you would probably know my style: being

---

[1] https://leanpub.com/practical-web-test-automation

practical. I will let the test scripts do the most talking. These recipe test scripts are 'live', as I have created web sites and offline web pages for testing. By using this book, sample test scripts and test pages (or sites), you can

1. **Identify** your issue
2. **Find** the recipe
3. **Run** the test case
4. **See** test execution in your browser

Who should read this book

Testers or programmers who write (or want to learn) Watir automated tests to test web applications.

How to read this book

Usually, a 'recipe' book is a reference book. Readers can go directly to the part that interests them. For example, if you are testing a multiple select list and don't know how, you can look up in the Table of Contents, then go to chapter 8. As software testing is so practical, testers can use this book to learn test automation in Watir too, by going through recipes one by one. I have arranged the recipes according to the levels of complexity.

Get recipe test scripts

To help readers learn more effectively, this book has a dedicated site[2] which contains the sample test scripts and related resources. The test scripts are packaged with sample web pages to make it easier and quicker for executing tests.

All recipe test scripts are Watir 7 compliant and run on all major browsers (*watir*: Chrome or Firefox on Windows, macOS and Linux, *watir-classic*: Internet Explorer 11 on Windows 10). I plan to keep the test scripts updated with the latest stable Watir version.

---

[2]http://zhimin.com/books/watir-recipes

Send me feedback

I would appreciate hearing from you. Comments, suggestions, errors in the book and test scripts are all welcome. You can submit your feedback on the book's site.

Zhimin Zhan

Brisbane, Australia

1. Introduction

Watir (Web Application Testing in Ruby) is a free and open source library for automated testing web applications in web browsers. I assume you already know something about Watir, simply based on the fact that you have picked up this book or opened it in your eBook reader.

1.1 Watir and its variants

The 'r' in Watir stands for 'Ruby', a free and powerful dynamic language with concise and elegant syntax. In other words, Watir test scripts are Ruby scripts. Inspired by Watir's success, there are clone frameworks in .NET and Java platforms: WatiN and Watij respectively. In my view, these two test frameworks are of not much value. There is a clear reason why creators of Watir included Ruby in the name, simply because of its importance (popular web framework Ruby on Rails also includes Ruby in its name). The concise, intuitiveness and flexibility of Ruby programming language makes it an ideal choice for automated test scripts. By the way, Ruby is a scripting language, Java and C# are not.

Watir-Classic

Watir Classic is a Watir driver for automating Internet Explorer on Windows. Watir-classic directly drives the browser through Microsoft's OLE protocol. The original Watir supports IE only, later, the *watir* gem was renamed to *watir-classic*.

The below is a simple *watir-classic* test script to open a new IE browser window and navigate to the Watir home page.

```
require 'watir-classic'
browser = Watir::Browser.new
browser.goto("http://watir.com")
```

Watir-WebDriver is new Watir

Watir-WebDriver is WebDriver-backed Watir, i.e. Watir syntax test scripts with Selenium-WebDriver as the engine underneath. One major benefit is that Watir-WebDriver test scripts can run on Chrome, Firefox, IE and Edge on multiple platforms including Windows, Linux and Mac. From version 6, Watir-WebDriver is the new Watir.

In theory, switching Watir-Classic to Watir (or vice versa) is as simple as changing the required library.

```
require 'watir'
browser = Watir::Browser.new
browser.goto("http://watir.com")
```

In this edition, I will focus on the new Watir, except a few recipes that are applicable only to Watir-Classic (and they are highlighted).

1.2 RSpec

Watir drives browsers, however, to make the effective use of Watir scripts for testing, we need to put them in a test framework which defines test structures and provides assertions (to perform checks in test scripts). Typical choices are:

- xUnit Unit Test Frameworks such as JUnit, NUnit.
- Behaviour Driven Frameworks such as RSpec, Cucumber.

In this book, I mainly use RSpec, the de facto Behaviour Driven Development (BDD) framework for Ruby.

```
describe "A grouped collection of test case " do
  before(:all) do
    @browser = Watir::Browser.new
  end

  after(:all) do
    browser.close unless debugging?
  end

  before(:each) do
    browser.goto(site_url)
  end

  # 'it' marks the start of a test case, ends with the matching 'end'
```

```
it "Check page title" do
  expect(browser.title).to eq("Watir Recipes")
  expect(browser.title.include?("Watir")).to be_truthy
  expect(browser.title.include?("Watir")).to be_falsey
  expect(browser.title).not_to include("Selenium")
end

# more test cases ...

end
```

The keywords `describe`, `before`, `after` and `it` define the structure of a test script.

- **describe "..." do**

  Description of a collection of related test cases
- **before()** and **after()**.

  Optional test statements run before and after each or all test cases.
- **it "..." do**

  Individual test case.

`expect(...).to` statements are called rspec-expectations, which are used to perform checks. There is also an older `should-based` syntax, which is still supported in RSpec but deprecated. Here is the `should-syntax` version of the above example:

```
browser.title.should == "Watir Recipes"
browser.title.include?("Watir").should be_truthy
browser.title.include?("Watir").should_not be_falsey
browser.title.should_not include("Selenium")
```

You will find more about RSpec from its home page[1]. However, I honestly don't think it is necessary. The part used for test scripts is not much and quite intuitive. After studying and trying out some examples, you will be quite comfortable with RSpec.

1.3 Run recipe scripts

Test scripts for all recipes can be downloaded from the book's site. They are all in ready-to-run state. I include the target web pages or sites as well as Watir test scripts. There are two kinds of target web pages: local HTML files and web pages on a live site.

---
[1]http://rspec.info

Run tests in TestWise

In this book, I refer to TestWise 6, a functional testing Integration Development Environment (IDE) that supports Watir and Selenium WebDriver, when editing or executing test scripts. If you have a preferred testing IDEs such as Aptana Studio and NetBeans 6 or code editors such as Sublime Text and TextMate, go for it. It shall not affect your learning this book or running recipe test scripts.

Installation of TestWise is easy. It only takes a couple of minutes to download and install. TestWise is the only software you need to use while learning with this book or developing Watir test scripts for your work.

To open recipe test scripts, close currently opened project (if there is one). Select menu File → Open Project,

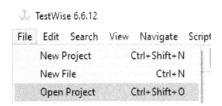

Select the project file *watir-recipes-sources\watir-recipes-samples.tpr*

The TestWise window shall appear as below:

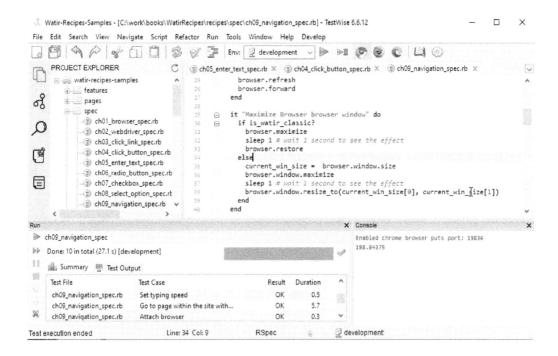

Find the test case

You can locate the recipe either by following the chapters or searching by names. There are over 160 test cases in one test project. Here is the quickest way to find the one you want in TestWise.

Select the menu 'Navigation' → 'Go to Test Case..'.

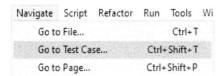

The "Go to Test Case" window appears with a list of the test cases from the project. The searching starts as you type.

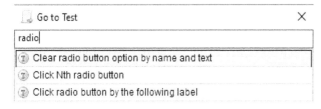

If you want to find a test case within a test script file, in the editor, press Ctrl+F12 to show and select a test case.

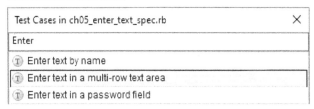

Run individual test case

Move the cursor to a line within a test case (between it "..." do and end). Right click and select Run '...'.

```
⊟    it "Verify checkbox is selected" do
         browser.checkbox(:name => "vehicle_bike").set
         expect(browser.checkbox(:name => "vehicle_bike").set?).to be_truthy
         browser.checkbox(:name => "vehicle_bike").click
         expect(browser.checkbox(:name => "vehicle_bike").set?).to be_falsey
     |
          ▷▤   Run "Verify checkbox is selected"              Ctrl+Shift+F10
     end  ▷    Run test cases in 'ch07_checkbox_spec'             Shift+F10
```

The below is a screenshot of execution panel when one test case failed,

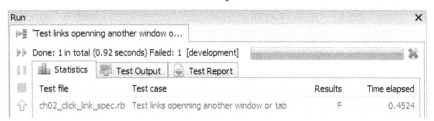

Run all test cases in a test script file

You can also run all test cases in currently opened test script file by clicking the blue triangle button on the top toolbar.

The below is a screenshot of the execution panel when all test cases in a test script file passed.

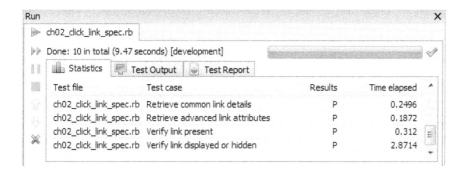

Run tests from command line

One advantage of open-source test frameworks, such as Watir and Selenium, is FREEDOM. You can edit the test scripts in any text editor and run them from a command line.

You will need to install Ruby first, then install RSpec and the preferred web test driver and library (known as Gem in Ruby). Basic steps are:

- install Ruby interpreter

  Window installer: http://rubyinstaller.org Linux or Mac: included or compile from source
- install RSpec

  > *gem install rspec*
- install test framework gem(s)

  > *gem install watir*

  or

  > *gem install watir-classic*

For windows users, you may simply download and install the free pre-packaged RubyShell (based on Ruby Windows Installer) at *http://testwisely.com/testwise/downloads*[2].

Once the installation is complete (it takes about 1 minute), we can run an RSpec test from the command line. You need to have some knowledge of typing commands in a console (Unix) or command prompt.

To run test cases in a test script file (e.g. google_spec.rb), enter the command

---

[2]http://testwisely.com/testwise/downloads

```
> rspec google_spec.rb
```

NOTE: remember to navigate or change the directory to the files' location.

Run multiple test script files in one go:

```
> rspec first_spec.rb   second_spec.rb
```

Run individual test case in a test script file, supply a line number in chosen test case range.

```
> rspec google_spec.rb:30
```

To generate a test report in HTML (under the current directory) after test execution:

```
> rspec -fh google_spec.rb > test_report.html
```

The command syntax is the same for Mac OS X and Linux platforms.

2. Watir and Selenium WebDriver

Watir (after version 6) is really an implementation built on Selenium WebDriver, in other words, Watir syntax on top of Selenium. Selenium WebDriver, aka Selenium 2, is another free and open-source web test automation library. Many like the simple and elegant syntax of Watir, but want to use Selenium's strength on multi-browser support. Watir-WebDriver fills the need. Then the original Watir is renamed to 'Watir-Classic' and 'Watir-WebDriver' is renamed to 'Watir'.

2.1 Install Selenium Browser Drivers

Different from `watir-classic` (drives only Internet Explorer on Windows platform), Watir can drive tests in all major browsers: Chrome, Firefox, IE and Edge on Windows, Mac and Linux platforms. Besides the browser itself, its corresponding driver server also needs to installed.

- ChromeDriver

  Download ChromeDriver[1] for your platform (Windows, macOS or Linux) and put `chromedriver` in a folder that is a part of your PATH environment variable. (the installation is the same for others

- GeckoDriver

  GeckoDriver[2] drives Firefox.
- Edge Driver

  Edge Driver[3] drives Microsoft Edge Chromium. The driver for the legacy Edge is called Microsoft WebDriver, which is now deprecated.
- IE Driver Server

  Download IE Driver Server[4] (choose 32bit or 64bit version based on your OS) and place it in a directory in PATH. Configuration is required for your IE browser depending its version, see IE and IEDriverServer Runtime Configuration[5] for details.

---

[1]https://sites.google.com/a/chromium.org/chromedriver/downloads
[2]https://github.com/mozilla/geckodriver/releases
[3]https://developer.microsoft.com/en-us/microsoft-edge/tools/webdriver/
[4]http://www.seleniumhq.org/download/
[5]https://code.google.com/p/selenium/wiki/InternetExplorerDriver#Required_Configuration

- Safari Driver, pre-installed

2.2 Cross browser testing with Watir

```
require 'watir'

describe "Same test on 4 different browsers" do

  it "Watir-WebDriver IE" do
    browser = Watir::Browser.new(:ie)
    browser.goto("http://testwisely.com/demo")
    browser.link(:text, "NetBank").click
    browser.text_field(:amount, "299" )
    browser.quit
  end

  it "Watir-WebDriver Firefox" do
    browser = Watir::Browser.new(:firefox)
    browser.goto("http://testwisely.com/demo")
    browser.link(:text, "NetBank").click
    browser.text_field(:amount, "299" )
    browser.quit
  end

  it "Watir-WebDriver Chrome" do
    browser = Watir::Browser.new(:chrome)
    browser.goto("http://testwisely.com/demo")
    browser.link(:text, "NetBank").click
    browser.text_field(:amount, "299" )
    browser.quit
  end

  it "Watir-WebDriver Edge" do
    browser = Watir::Browser.new(:edge)
    browser.goto("http://testwisely.com/demo")
    browser.link(:text, "NetBank").click
    browser.text_field(:amount, "299" )
    browser.quit
  end

end
```

Please note that the execution of IE in Watir is different from Watir-Classic, which is based on OLE.

2.3 Selenium WebDriver Locators

As you might have already figured out, to drive an element in a page, we need to find it first. Selenium WebDriver uses what is called locators to find and match the elements on web page. There are 9 locators in Selenium:

Locator	Example
ID	`find_element(:id, "user")`
Name	`find_element(:name, "username")`
Link Text	`find_element(:link_text, "Login")`
	`find_element(:link, "Login")`
Partial Link Text	`find_element(:partial_link_text, "Next")`
XPath	`find_element(:xpath,`
	`"//div[@id="login"]/input")`
Tag Name	`find_element(:tag_name, "body")`
Class Name	`find_element(:class_name, "table")`
	`find_element(:class, "body")`
CSS	`find_element(:css, "#login >`
	`input[type="text"]")`
Relative (v4)	`find_element(relative: { tag_name: "img",`
	`right: elem })`

You may use any one of them to narrow down the element you are looking for.

Here is a sample Selenium-WebDriver test script.

```
driver = Selenium::WebDriver.for(:chrome)
driver.navigate.to("http://travel.agileway.net")
driver.find_element(id: "username").send_keys("agileway")
driver.find_element(name: "password").send_keys("testwise")
driver.find_element(xpath: "//input[@value='Sign in']").click
```

2.4 Locating elements in Watir

Different from Selenium's generic approach of using `find_element` to locate a control on a web page, Watir syntax is based control types.

```
browser = Watir::Browser.new(:chrome)
browser.goto("http://travel.agileway.net")
browser.text_field(id: "username").set("agileway")
browser.text_field(name: "password").set(password)
browser.button(value: "Sign in").click
```

You can use the same way for most of HTML controls, including display only tags such
label and span. The full list is available on docs[6].

What about non-standard tag?

If the control you refer to is not in the above tag list or simply you don't care the tag, you
may just use element.

```
browser.element(id: "not_standard_tag")
```

Convert Watir Element to Selenium Element

```
watir_elem = browser.text_field(id: "username")
selenium_elem = watir_elem.wd
```

By converting to a Selenium element, you can use its functions[7].

2.5 Access underneath Selenium API

To master Watir, in my opinion, it is necessary to understand the underneath library:
Selenium WebDriver. We can use Selenium API directly using driver like the example
below:

---

[6]http://watir.github.io/watir-webdriver/doc/Watir/Container.html
[7]https://github.com/SeleniumHQ/selenium/blob/master/rb/lib/selenium/webdriver/common/element.rb

```
browser = Watir::Browser.new(:chrome)
browser.goto("http://testwisely.com/demo")
browser.driver.manage().window().resize_to(1024, 768) # Selenium
browser.driver.find_element(link_text: "NetBank").click
browser.select_list(name: "account").select("Savings") # Watir
browser.driver.find_element(name: "amount").send_keys("299") # Selenium
browser.button(value: "Transfer").click
browser.quit
```

For more Selenium examples, you may check out Selenium WebDriver Recipes in Ruby[8].

---

[8]https://leanpub.com/selenium-recipes-in-ruby

3. Hyperlink

Hyperlinks (or links) are fundamental elements of web pages. As a matter of fact, it is hyperlinks that makes the World Wide Web possible. A sample link is provided below, along with the HTML source.

Recommend Watir

HTML Source

```
<a href="index.html" id="like_watir_link" class="nav" data-id="1">Like Watir</a>
```

3.1 Start browser

Testing a website starts with opening a browser.

```
browser = Watir::Browser.new
browser.goto("http://testwisely.com/testwise")
```

 Watir-Classic

Watir-Classic may use `browser.start` as well.

```
browser = Watir::Browser.new
browser.start("http://testwisely.com/demo")
```

3.2 Click a link by text

Using text is probably the most direct way to click a link in Watir, as it is what we see on the page.

```
browser.link(text: "Like Watir").click
```

Click a link by ID

Using IDs is the easiest and the safest way to locate an element in HTML. If the page is W3C HTML conformed[1], the IDs should be unique and identified in web controls. In comparison to texts, test scripts that use IDs are less prone to application changes (e.g. an application designer or developer may decide to change the label, but less likely to change the ID).

```
browser.link(id: "sign_in_link").click
```

Furthermore, if you are testing a web site with multiple languages, using IDs is probably the only feasible option. You do not want to write test scripts like below:

```
if is_chinese?  # a helper function determines the locale
  browser.link(text: "██").click
elsif is_italian?
  browser.link(text: "Accedi").click
else
  browser.link(text: "Sign in").click
end
```

Click a link by partial text

Watir allows you to identify a hyperlink control with a partial text. This can be quite useful when the text is dynamically generated. In other words, the text on one web page might be different on your next visit. We might be able to use the common text shared by these dynamically generated link texts to identify them.

---

[1]http://www.w3.org/TR/WCAG20-TECHS/H93.html

```
browser.link(text: /partial/i).click  # contains 'partial', case insensitive
expect(browser.text).to include("This is partial link page")

# alternate should-syntax, however, not recommended
browser.text.should include("This is partial link page")
```

Here we use the regular expression in ("/.../"), a powerful pattern matching language. If you are not familiar with the regular expression, don't feel intimidated. The use of regular expression in automated test scripts is very minimal. Online regular expression testers such as Rubular[2] will make it easy to learn what you need.

By URL

This syntax (works in Watir-Classic) is really unnecessary, it has been removed in Watir.

```
browser.link(url: "http://testwisely.com/demo").click
```

3.3 Click Nth link with the same link text

It is not uncommon that there are more than one link with exactly the same text. By default, Watir will choose the first one. What if you want to click the second or Nth one?

The web page below contains three 'Show Answer" links,

1. Do you think automated testing is important and valuable? Show Answer

2. Why didn't you do automated testing in your projects previously? Show Answer

3. Your project now has so comprehensive automated test suite, What changed? Show Answer

To click the second one,

```
browser.link(:text => "Show Answer", :index => 1).click
```

The :index tells Watir which element to select in appearing order, Watir (since version 2.0) uses 0-based indexing, i.e. the first one is 0.

---

[2]http://rubular.com/

```
browser.link(text: "Show Answer").click  # this will click first link
browser.link(:text => "Show Answer", :index => 0).click # still first link
```

If there are multiple links with the same text that have different attribute values, such as 'class', we could use the attribute to narrow down the choice, such as

```
browser.link(:text => "Same link", :class => "small").click
```

3.4 Verify a link present or not?

```
expect(browser.link(text: "Sign in").present?).to be_truthy
expect(browser.link(id: "sign_out_link").present?).not_to be_truthy
```

Besides present?, you may use visible? to check whether an element is visible on the page.

```
browser.link(text: "Hide").click
expect(browser.link(text: "Like Watir").present?).to be_falsey
expect(browser.link(text: "Like Watir").visible?).to be_falsey
```

Watir-Classic

Watir-Classic also has another similar method exists?.

3.5 Getting link data attributes

Once a control is identified, we can get its other attributes of the element. This is generally applicable to most of the controls.

```
expect(browser.link(text: "Like Watir").href).to eq(site_url.gsub("link.html", "index.htm\
l"))
expect(browser.link(text: "Like Watir").id).to eq("like_watir_link")
expect(browser.link(id: "like_watir_link").text).to eq("Like Watir")
expect(browser.link(id: "like_watir_link").tag_name).to eq("a")
```

Also you can get the value of custom attributes of this element,

```
expect(browser.link(id: "like_watir_link").attribute_value("data-id")).to eq("123")
```

and its inline CSS style.

```
expect(browser.link(id: "like_watir_link").attribute_value("style")).to eq("font-size: 14\
px;")
```

Watir-Classic

A note on the 'style' attribute: the syntax is different between Watir-Classic and Watir.

```
expect(browser.link(id: "like_watir_link").style).to eq("font-size: 14px;")
# Please note using attribute_value("style") won't work in Watir-Classic
```

3.6 Test links open a new browser window

Clicking the link below will open the linked URL in a new browser window or tab.

```
<a href="http://testwisely.com/demo" target="_blank">Open new window</a>
```

For Watir-Classic, we could use attach method (see chapter 10) to find the new browser/tab window, it will be easier to perform all testing within one browser window. Here is how:

```
current_url = browser.url
new_window_url = browser.link(text: "Open new window").href
browser.goto(new_window_url)
# ... testing on new site
browser.text_field(name: "name").set "sometext"
browser.goto(current_url) # back
```

In this test script, we use a local variable (a programming term) 'current_url' to store the current URL.

4. Button

Buttons can come in two forms - standard and submit buttons. Standard buttons are usually created by the 'button' tag, whereas submit buttons are created by the 'input' tag (normally within form controls).

Standard button

Choose Watir

Submit button in a form

Username: Submit

HTML Source

```
<button id="choose_watir_btn" class="nav" data-id="123" style="font-size: 14px;">Choose W\
atir</button>
<!-- ... -->
<form name="input" action="index.html" method="get">
  Username: <input type="text" name="user">
  <input type="submit" name="submit_action" value="Submit">
</form>
```

Please note that some buttons are actually not buttons, but are hyperlinks styled by CSS.

4.1 Click a button by text

```
browser.button(value: "Choose Watir").click
```

For an input button (in a HTML input tag) in a form, the text shown on the button is the 'value' attribute which might contain extra spaces or invisible characters. Watir expects an exact match when searching an input control by value.

```
<input type="submit" name="submit_action" value="Space After "/>
```

```
# the below will fail
# browser.button(value: "Space After").click
browser.button(value: "Space After ").click
```

4.2 Click a button by ID

As always, a better way to identify a button is to use IDs. This applies to all controls.

```
browser.button(id: "choose_watir_btn").click
```

4.3 Click a button by name

For an input button, we can use a new generic attribute name to locate the control.

```
browser.button(name: "choose_watir").click
```

4.4 Click an image button

There is also another type of 'button': an image that works as a submit button in a form.

```
<input type="image" src="images/go.gif">
```

Besides using ID, the button can be identified by using :src attribute.

```
browser.button(src: /go/).click
```

/go/ is a regular expression, it means to locate a button whose src attribute contains 'go'.

4.5 Assert a button present

Just like hyperlinks, we can use present? to check whether a control is present on a web page. This check applies to most of the web controls in Watir.

```
expect(browser.button(text: "Choose Watir").present?).to be_truthy
expect(browser.button(text: "Choose Selenium").present?).not_to be_truthy
expect(browser.button(id: "choose_watir_btn").present?).to be_truthy
```

4.6 Assert a button displayed or hidden?

```
expect(browser.button(id: "choose_watir_btn").visible?).to be_truthy
expect(browser.button(text: "Choose Watir").visible?).to be_falsey
```

4.7 Assert a button enabled or disabled?

A web control can be in a disabled state. A disabled button is un-clickable, and it is displayed differently.

Choose Watir

Normally enabling or disabling buttons (or other web controls) are triggered by JavaScript.

```
expect(browser.button(text: "Choose Watir").enabled?).to be_truthy
browser.link(:text, "Disable").click
sleep 0.5
expect(browser.button(id: " choose_watir_btn").enabled?).to be_falsey
browser.link(:text, "Enable").click
sleep 1
expect(browser.button(id: " choose_watir_btn").enabled?).to be_truthy
```

5. TextField and TextArea

Text fields are commonly used in a form to pass user entered text data to the server. There are two variants (prior to HTML5): password fields and text areas. The characters in password fields are masked (shown as asterisks or circles). Text areas allows multiple lines of texts.

HTML Source

```
Username: <input type="text" name="username" id="user"><br>
Password: <input type="password" name="password" id="pass"> <br/>
Comments: <br/>
<textarea id="comments" rows="2" cols="60" name="comments"></textarea>
```

5.1 Enter text into a text field by name

```
browser.text_field(name: "username").set("new value")
```

The 'name' attribute is the identification used by programmers to process data, and it applies to all the web controls in a standard web form.

5.2 Enter text into a text field by ID

```
browser.text_field(id: "user").send_keys("tester1")
```

send_keys populates data in a text field. Commonly, testers tend to treat send_keys the same as set, but they are different. set clears the text field before populating the text while send_keys just send keys into text boxes. See the example below:

```
browser.text_field(id: "user").set("userone")
browser.text_field(id: "user").set("usertwo")
# Now value of this text box is 'usertwo'
browser.text_field(id: "user").clear
browser.text_field(id: "user").send_keys("userone")
browser.text_field(id: "user").send_keys("usertwo")
# The value in text field might have different values
# depends on your IE browser version, the value can be
#'useroneusertwo', 'userone', 'useroneo' (don't ask me why)
```

5.3 Enter text into a password field

In Watir, password text fields are treated as normal text fields, except that the entered text is masked.

```
browser.text_field(id: "pass").set("testisfun")
```

HTML5 introduces some new text input controls such as e-mail address (type='email') and number (type='number') input fields. They are also treated as normal input text fields in Watir.

5.4 Clear a text field

```
browser.text_field(id: "user").set("testwisely")
browser.text_field(name: "username").clear
```

5.5 Enter text into a multi-line text area

```
browser.textarea(id: "comments").set("Automated testing is\r\nFun!")
```

The "\r\n" represents a new line.

5.6 Assert value

```
browser.text_field(id: "user").set("testwisely")
expect(browser.text_field(id: "user").value).to eq("testwisely")
```

5.7 Focus on a control

Once we identify a control in Watir, we can set the focus on it.

```
browser.text_field(id: "user").focus
```

5.8 Set a value to a read-only or disabled text field

'Read only' and 'disabled' text fields are not editable and are shown differently in the browser (typically grayed out).

```
Readonly text field:
<input type="text" name="readonly_text" readonly="true"/> <br/>
Disabled text field:
<input type="text" name="disabled_text" disabled="true"/>
```

If a text box is set to be read-only, the following test step won't work.

```
browser.text_field(name: "readonly_text").set("new value")
```

Watir-Classic

Here is a workaround:

```
browser.text_field(name: "readonly_text").value = "anyuse" # OK
browser.text_field(name: "disabled_text").value = "bypass" # OK
```

Watir-WebDriver

The above method `value =` does not work for Watir-WebDriver. But there is another workaround:

```
browser.execute_script("$('#readonly_text').val('bypass');")
expect(browser.text_field(name: "readonly_text").value).to eq("bypass")
browser.execute_script("$('#disabled_text').val('anyuse');")
expect(browser.text_field(name: "disabled_text").value).to eq("anyuse")
```

Below is a screenshot of a disabled and read-only text fields that were 'injected' with two
values from the above test script.

Disabled text field: anyuse
Readonly text field: bypass

6. Radio button

⦿ Male
○ Female

HTML Source

```
<input type="radio" name="gender" value="male" id="radio_male" checked="true">Male<br>
<input type="radio" name="gender" value="female" id="radio_female">Female
```

6.1 Select radio button by name and value

```
browser.radio(:name => "gender", :value => "male").click
```

The radio buttons in the same radio group have the same name. To click a radio option, its value needs to be specified. Please note that the value is not the text shown next to the radio button. To find out the value of a radio button, inspect the HTML source.

6.2 Select radio button by ID

```
browser.radio(id: "radio_female").click
```

6.3 Clear radio option selection

Watir Classic

```
browser.radio(:name => "gender", :value => "female").clear
```

Watir

There is no `clear` method for Watir. To clear one radio button, you will need to select another one.

The above example clears the selected radio option. If the radio option is not selected, no error will be thrown.

6.4 Assert a radio option is selected

The below script ensures the radio button is selected.

```
browser.radio(:name => "gender", :value => "male").set # same as click
expect(browser.radio(:name => "gender", :value => "male").set?).to be_truthy
```

6.5 Iterate radio buttons in a radio group

So far we have been focusing on identifying web controls by using one type of locator such as `text_field` and `radio`. Here I will introduce another type of Watir locators (I call them plural locators).

```
expect(browser.radios(:name => "gender").size).to eq(2)
browser.radios(:name => "gender").each do |rb|
  rb.click if rb.value == "female"
end
```

The difference between `radio` and `radios` is that `radio` only returns one matched element, whereas `radios` return a list of them (also known as an array). Similar methods are

- links
- buttons
- text_fields
- checkboxes
- select_lists

Although these Watir methods are not frequently used, they can be quite handy especially when elements are hard to locate. There was once I was performing tests an online calendar, there were many time-slots and the HTML for each of these time-slots were exactly the same. I simply identified the time slot by using the index (as below) on one of these 'plural' locators.

```
browser.radios[1].click # click the second radio button on the page
```

7. CheckBox

☐ I have a bike
☑ I have a car

HTML Source

```
<input type="checkbox" name="vehicle_bike" value="on" id="checkbox_bike">I have a bike<br>
<input type="checkbox" name="vehicle_car" id="checkbox_car">I have a car
```

7.1 Select by name

```
browser.checkbox(:name => "vehicle_bike").set
browser.checkbox(name: "vehicle_car").set
```

The above two test statements work identically. You may additional attributes such as:

```
# Check the second with the same name
browser.checkbox(name: "vehicle_bike", index: 1).set
```

7.2 Select by ID

```
browser.checkbox(id: "checkbox_car").set
```

You may also use `click` function, which is equivalent to a mouse click on a check box, i.e. toggle the checkbox's state.

7.3 Uncheck a checkbox

```
browser.checkbox(:name => "vehicle_bike").set
browser.checkbox(:id => "checkbox_bike").clear
```

Calling clear on an unchecked checkbox does not throw errors, it will have no effect.

7.4 Assert a checkbox is checked (or not)

```
browser.checkbox(:name => "vehicle_bike").set
expect(browser.checkbox(:name => "vehicle_bike").set?).to be_truthy
browser.checkbox(:name => "vehicle_bike").click
expect(browser.checkbox(:name => "vehicle_bike").set?).to be_falsey
```

8. Select List

A Select list is also known as a drop-down list or combobox.

HTML Source

```
<select name="car_make" id="car_make_select">
  <option value="">-- Select --</option>
  <option value="honda">Honda (Japan)</option>
  <option value="volvo">Volvo (Sweden)</option>
  <option value="audi">Audi (Germany)</option>
</select>
```

8.1 Select an option by text or value

```
browser.select_list(:name => "car_make").select("Volvo (Sweden)")
# or
browser.select_list(name: "car_make").select("volvo")
```

The texts within a select list is what we see in the browser and the value is what to be passed to the server. In Watir, the 'select' function will accept either text or value.

Works for watir

```
browser.select_list(id: "car_make_select").select(value: "audi")
```

Works for watir-classic only

```
browser.select_list(id: "car_make_select").select_value("audi")
```

I would advise to use one way consistently.

8.2 Select an option by ID

```
browser.select_list(id: "car_make_select").select("Honda (Japan)")
```

8.3 Select an option by iterating all options

Here I will show you a more complex way to select an option in a select list, not for the sake of complexity, of course. A select list contains options, where each option itself is a valid control in Watir.

```
car_make_options = browser.select_list(id: "car_make_select").options
car_make_options.each do |co|
  if co.text == "Volvo (Sweden)"
    co.select
    break
  end
end
```

8.4 Select multiple options

A select list also supports multiple selections.

Framework:

HTML Source

```
<select id="framework_select" name="test_framework" multiple="multiple">
  <option></option>
  <option value="rwebspec">RWebSpec</option>
  <option value="watir">Watir</option>
  <option value="selenium">Selenium</option>
</select>
```

```
browser.select_list(name: 'test_framework').select('Watir')
browser.select_list(name: 'test_framework').select('RWebSpec')
```

8.5 Clear selection

Clear selection works the same way for both single and multiple select lists.

```
browser.select_list(id: "car_make_select").clear
browser.select_list(name: "test_framework").clear
```

8.6 Assert selected option

To verify an option is selected in a select list:

```
browser.select_list(id: "car_make_select").select(value: "audi")

# only works for label not value
expect(browser.select_list(id: "car_make_select").selected?("Audi (Germany)")).to be_trut\
hy

# another way
expect(browser.select_list(id: "car_make_select").selected_options.size).to eq(1)
expect(browser.select_list(id: "car_make_select").selected_options[0].text).to eq("Audi (\
Germany)")
expect(browser.select_list(id: "car_make_select").selected_options[0].value).to eq("audi")
```

8.7 Assert the value of a select list

Another quick and simple way to check the selected value of a select list:

```
expect(browser.select_list(id: "car_make_select").value).to eq("")
browser.select_list(id: "car_make_select").select_value("audi")
expect(browser.select_list(id: "car_make_select").value).to eq("audi")
```

8.8 Assert option text in a select list

```
expect( browser.select_list(id: "car_make_select").include?("Audi (Germany)") ).to be_tru\
thy
expect( browser.select_list(id: "car_make_select")).to include("Honda (Japan)")
# work for value as well, changed from previous versions
browser.select_list(id: "car_make_select").include?("audi") # => true
```

8.9 Assert multiple selections

A multiple select list can have multiple options being selected.

```
browser.select_list(name: 'test_framework').select('Watir')
browser.select_list(name: 'test_framework').select('RWebSpec')
selected =  browser.select_list(name: 'test_framework').selected_options
expect(selected.size).to eq(2)
expect(selected[0].text).to eq("RWebSpec") # option display order
expect(selected[1].text).to eq("Watir")
```

Although the test script selected 'Watir' first, when it comes to assertion, the first selected option will be 'RWebSpec', not 'Watir'.

9. Navigation and Browser

Driving common web controls were covered from chapters 2 to 7. In this chapter, I will show how to manage browser windows and page navigation in them.

9.1 Go to a URL

```
browser.goto("http://itest2.com")
browser.goto("https://testwisely.com/demo")
```

9.2 Go to pages within the site without specifying full URL

`browser.goto` takes a full URL. Most of time, testers test against a single site and specifying a full URL (such as http://...) is not necessary. We can create a reusable function to simplify its usage.

```
$site_root_url = "http://test.testwisely.com"

# ...

def visit(path)
 browser.goto("#{$site_root_url}#{path}")
end

it "Go to page within the site" do
  visit("/demo")
  visit("/demo/survey")
  visit("/")  # home page
end
```

Apart from being more readable, there is another benefit with this approach. If you want to run the same test against at a different server (the same application deployed on another machine), you only need to make one change: the value of `$site_root_url`.

```
$site_root_url = "http://dev.testwisely.com"
```

9.3 Perform actions from right click context menu such as 'Back', 'Forward' or 'Refresh'

Operations with right click context menu are commonly page navigations, such as "Back to previous page". We can achieve the same by calling the test framework's navigation operations directly.

```
browser.back
browser.refresh
browser.forward
```

9.4 Maximize browser window

```
current_win_size =  browser.window.size
browser.window.maximize
sleep 1
browser.window.resize_to(current_win_size[0], current_win_size[1])
```

 ## Watir-Classic: Maximize IE window

```
browser.maximize
sleep 1 # wait 1 second to see the effect
browser.restore
```

9.5 Minimize browser window

As far as I know, Watir-WebDriver does support browser minimization. The below is a hack to achieve the similar outcome.

```
browser.window.move_to(-3000, 0)
sleep 1
browser.window.move_to(0, 0)
```

While the browser's window is minimized, the test execution still can run.

 Watir-Classic: minimize IE window

```
browser.minimize
sleep 1 # wait 1 second to see the effect
browser.restore
```

9.6 Set typing speed

 Watir-Classic only

In Watir, the speed of populating data in text fields is very fast. The speed can be adjusted with one of the following options:

1. zippy (the fastest)
2. fast
3. slow

```
browser.link(text: "Text Field").click
browser.speed = :slow # or :zippy, :fast
browser.text_field(name: "username").set "a very long time"
```

Watir-WebDriver

In watir-webdriver, there is no built-in function to control the speed of populating data. However, you can modify your test script to adjust the speed for the 'send_keys' function.

9.7 Attaching browser

 Watir-Classic only

Watir-Classic has a convenient way to switch between browsers by invoking the method 'attach'. This is a very useful feature for testing, which will be covered more in the debugging chapter.

The following attributes can be used to identify the browser when invoking 'attach'.

- title
- url
- index

```
existing_browser = Watir::Browser.attach(:title, "TestWisely")
existing_browser.maximize

another_browser = Watir::Browser.attach(:url, "http://watir.com/")
another_browser.link(text: "Installation").click

first_browser = Watir::Browser.attach(:index, 0)
#...
```

9.8 Reuse browser

 Watir-Classic only

When executing the samples test scripts, you may have noticed that every test starts with a new browser instance and then closes after each execution. For example:

```
before(:all) do
  @browser = Watir::Browser.new
end

# ...

after(:all) do
  browser.close unless debugging?
end
```

To speed up the test execution, we can reuse the existing browser to perform the next set of tests. I prefer this approach as there is no overhead of starting and closing browsers.

```
before(:all) do
  @browser  = nil
  Watir::Browser.each do |ie_win|
    @browser = ie_win
    break
  end
  # if not found create a new one
  @browser ||= Watir::Browser.new
  @browser.goto(site_url)
end

after(:all) do
  # we don't close browser if want to adope browser reuse
  # @browser.close unless debugging?
end

it "Test Case" do
  @browser.link(text: "Hyperlink").click
end
```

If adopting this approach, remember not to close the browser after each test execution.

9.9 Resizing browser window

Window resizing is only supported in Watir-WebDriver, not in Watir-Classic (let me know if you have found a workaround). In Watir-WebDriver, you can resize or move the browser as below.

```
browser.window.resize_to(800, 600)
# and you can move the browser
browser.window.move_to(0, 0)
```

So how do we ensure we are testing with the appropriate window size in Classic Watir? My answer is simple. Simply adjust the window size at the time the new browser window is opened. You can reuse the same browser for other tests (please refer to 'Reuse browser' in the above section)

9.10 Remember current web page URL, then come back to it later

We can store the page's URL to an instance variable (@url, for example).

```
before(:all) do
  open_browser("http://testwisely.com/demo")
  @url = browser.url
end

it "Go to other pages then go back directly to remembered URL" do
  browser.link(text: "NetBank").click
  browser.goto(@url)
end
```

In previous chapters, local variables were used to store values for later use. So why do some variables have an '@' symbol in front? This is to show that the variable can be used anywhere within the test script file, and not specifically to a block of tests (typically between it "..." do to end).

In the example above, the url variable is defined in before(:all) scope. To make it accessible to the test cases in the test script file, it is defined as an instance variable: @url.

9.11 Scroll to the bottom of a page

Calling JavaScript API.

```
browser.goto("https://clinicwise.net/pricing") # a long page
browser.execute_script("window.scrollTo(0, document.body.scrollHeight);")
```

Or send the keyboard command: 'Ctrl+End'.

```
browser.body.send_keys([:control, :end])
```

9.12 Scroll to focus on a control

For certain controls are not viewable in a web page, WebDriver unable to click on them by returning an error like *"Element is not clickable at point (1180, 43)"*. The solution is to scroll the browser view to the control.

```
browser.goto(site_url + "/button.html") # a long page
browser.window.resize_to(640, 180)

elem = browser.button(name: "submit_action_2")
elem_pos = elem.wd.location["y"]
puts elem_pos
browser.execute_script("window.scroll(0, #{elem_pos})")
sleep(1)
elem.click()
```

9.13 Switch browser or tab

```
browser.link(text: "Hyperlink").click
browser.link(text: "Open new window").click # target='_blank' link
browser.windows.wait_until(size: 2)
# switch to the last tab
# browser.windows.last.use # does not work in Watir 7
browser.switch_window
expect(browser.text).to include("This is url link page")

# back to first tab
browser.switch_window
expect(browser.link(text: "Open new window").present?).to be_truthy
```

10. Assertion

Without assertions (often known as checks), a test case is incomplete. Common assertions for testing web applications are:

- page title (equals)
- page text (contains or does not contain)
- page source (contains or does not contain)
- input element value (equals)
- display element text (equals)
- element state (selected, disabled, displayed)

10.1 Assert page title

```
expect(browser.title).to eq("TestWise IDE")
```

10.2 Assert page text

Example web page

```
Text assertion with a  (tab before), and
(new line before)!
```

HTML source

```
<PRE>Text assertion with a  (<b>tab</b> before), and
(new line before)!</PRE>
```

Test script

```
matching_str = "Text assertion with a  (tab before), and \r\n(new line before)!"
expect(browser.text).to include(matching_str)
```

Non Windows platform

Use '\n' instead of '\r\n' for new line characters.

```
matching_str = "Text assertion with a  (tab before), and \n(new line before)!"
expect(browser.text).to include(matching_str)
```

Please note the browser.text returns the text of a web page after stripping off the HTML tags, but may not exactly the same as we saw on the browser.

10.3 Assert page source

The page source is raw HTML returned from the server.

```
expect(browser.html).to include("Text assertion with a  (<b>tab</b> before), and \n(new l\
ine before)!")
```

IE (before IE10)

Tag names are in upper case for old IE versions.

```
expect(browser.html).to include("Text assertion with a  (<B>tab</B> before), and \r\n(new\
 line before)!")
```

10.4 Assert browser status

IE's status message is the text displayed at the bottom of a browser window. Its text may be set by the browser after loading a page or JavaScript. This message can be used for assertion.

If a page is loaded successfully, the status text is empty in IE9 ('Done' in IE8).

```
expect(browser.status).to eq("")  # IE9 default
# loading a new page with customised text message
browser.link(text: "Change status message").click
sleep 1
expect(browser.status).to eq("Test Automation is Fun!")
```

10.5 Assert label text

HTML source

```
<label id="receipt_number">NB123454</label>
```

Label tags are commonly used in web pages to wrap texts. It can be quite useful to assert a specific text.

```
expect(browser.label(id: "receipt_number").text).to eq("NB123454")
```

10.6 Assert span text

HTML source

```
<span id="span_2">Second Span</span>
```

From testing perspectives, spans are the same as labels, only with a different tag name.

```
expect(browser.span(id: "span_2").text).to eq("Second Span")
```

10.7 Assert div text or HTML

Example page

Wise Products
TestWise
BuildWise

HTML source

```
<div id="div_parent">
   Wise Products
   <div id="div_child_1">
            TestWise
   </div>
   <div id="div_child_2">
            BuildWise
   </div>
 </div>
```

Test script

```
expect(browser.div(id: "div_child_1").text).to eq("TestWise")
expect(browser.div(id: "div_parent").text).to eq("Wise Products \r\nTestWise \r\nBuildWis\
e")
```

10.8 Assert table text

HTML tables are commonly used for displaying grid data on web pages.

Example page

A	B
a	b

HTML source

```
<table id="aha_table" cellpadding="1" border="1" width="30%">
  <tr id="row_1">
    <td id="cell_1_1">A</td>
    <td id="cell_1_2">B</td>
  </tr>
  <tr id="row_2">
    <td id="cell_2_1">a</td>
    <td id="cell_2_2">b</td>
  </tr>
</table>
```

Test script

```
expect(browser.table(id: "alpha_table").text).to eq("AB\r\nab")
browser.table(id: "alpha_table").html.should include("<td id=\"cell_1_1\">A</td>")
# before IE10
# browser.table(id: "alpha_table").html.should include("<TD id=cell_1_1>A</TD>")
```

Non-IE Browsers

```
expect(browser.table(id: "alpha_table").text).to eq("A B\na b")
browser.table(id: "alpha_table").html.should include("<td id=\"cell_1_1\">A</td>"
```

10.9 Assert text in a table cell

If a table cell (td tag) has a unique ID, we can locate it by using td method in Watir.

```
expect(browser.td(id: "cell_1_1").text).to eq("A")
```

An alternative approach is to identify a table cell by using row and column indexes (both starting with 0).

```
expect(browser.table(id: "alpha_table")[1][1].text).to eq("b")
```

10.10 Assert text in a table row

```
browser.tr(id: "row_1").text.should == "AB"
```

10.11 Assert image present

```
expect(browser.image(id: "next_go").exists?).to be_truthy
```

11. Frames

HTML Frames are treated as independent pages, which is not a good web design practice. As a result, few new sites use frames nowadays. However, there a quite a number of sites that uses iframes.

11.1 Testing Frames

Here is a layout of a fairly common frame setup: navigations on the top, menus on the left and the main content on the right.

HTML Source

```
<frameset rows="100,*" frameborder="0" border="0" framespacing="0">
  <frame name="topNav" src="top_nav.html">
  <frameset cols="200,*" frameborder="0" border="0" framespacing="0">
    <frame name="menu" id="menu_frame" src="menu_1.html" marginheight="0" marginwidth="0"\
 scrolling="auto" noresize>
    <frame name="content" src="content.html" marginheight="0" marginwidth="0" scrolling="\
auto" noresize>
  </frameset>
</frameset>
```

To test a frame with Watir, we need to identify the frame first, by ID, NAME or SRC.

```
browser.goto(site_url + "/frames.html")
expect(browser.frames.count).to eq(3)
browser.frame(name: "topNav").link(:text, "Menu 2 in top frame").click
browser.frame(id: "menu_frame").link(:text, "Green Page").click
puts browser.frames[2].src

browser.frame(src: /content/).link(:text, "Back to original page").click
```

This script clicks a link in each of three frames: top, menu and content.

11.2 Testing iframe

An iframe (Inline Frame) is a web page embedded inside another web page.

Example page

Enter name:

Username:
Password:
Login

□ I accept terms and conditions

HTML Source

```
<IFRAME frameborder='1' id="Frame1" src="login_iframe.html"
        Style="HEIGHT: 100px; WIDTH: 320px; MARGIN=0" SCROLLING="no" >
</IFRAME>
```

The test script below enters text in the main page, fills the sign in form in an iframe, and ticks the checkbox on the main page:

```
browser.goto(site_url + "/iframe.html")
expect(browser.iframes.count).to eq(1)
expect(browser.frames.count).to eq(0) # frame is different from iframe
browser.text_field(name: "user").set("agileway")
browser.iframe(id: "Frame1").text_field(name: "username").set("tester")
browser.iframe(id: "Frame1").text_field(name: "password").set("TestWise")
browser.iframe(id: "Frame1").button(value: "Login").click
sleep 1
expect(browser.iframe(id: "Frame1").html).to include("Signed in")
# back to main body
browser.checkbox(id: "accept_terms").set
```

After test execution, the web page will appear like below:

The content of the iframe changed, but not the main page.

11.3 Test multiple iframes

A web page may contain multiple iframes.

```
browser.goto(site_url + "/iframes.html")
expect(browser.iframes.size).to eq(2)
browser.iframe(index: 0).text_field(name: "username").set("agileway")
browser.iframe(index: 1).radio(id: "radio_male").set
```

We may use other attribute such as src to locate an iframe:

```
browser.iframe(src: /radio_button/).radio(id: "radio_female").set
```

12. Testing AJAX

AJAX (an acronym for Asynchronous JavaScript and XML) is widely used in web sites nowadays. Let's look at an example first:

NetBank

To Account: Savings

Enter Amount: 1200

[Transfer]

On clicking 'Transfer' button, an animated loading image showed up indicating 'transfer in progress'.

NetBank

To Account: Savings

Enter Amount: 1200

[Transfer]

Receipt No: 9010
Receipt Date: **02/01/2015**

After the server processing the request, the loading image is gone and a receipt number is displayed.

From testing perspective, a test step (like clicking 'Transfer' button) is completed immediately. However the updates to parts of a web page may happen after unknown delay, which differs from traditional web requests.

There are 2 common ways to test AJAX operations: waiting enough time or checking the web page periodically for a maximum given time.

12.1 Wait within a time frame

After triggering an AJAX operation (clicking a link or button, for example), we can set a timer in our test script to wait for all the asynchronous updates to occur before executing next step.

```
browser.goto("http://testwisely.com/demo/netbank")
browser.button(:value,"Transfer").click  # AJAX
sleep 10
expect(browser.text).to include("Receipt No:")
```

`sleep 10` means waiting for 10 seconds, after clicking 'Transfer' button. 10 seconds later, the test script will check for the 'Receipt No:' text on the page. If the text is present, the test passes; otherwise, the test fails. In other words, if the server finishes the processing and return the results correctly in 11 seconds, this test would fail.

12.2 Explicit Waits until Time out

Apparently, the waiting for a specified time is not ideal. If the operation finishes earlier, the test execution would still be on halt. Instead of passively waiting, we can write test scripts to define a wait statement for certain condition to be satisfied until the wait reaches its timeout period. If Watir finds the element before the defined timeout value, the code execution will continue to next line of code.

```
browser.button(value: "Transfer").click
Watir::Wait.until{ browser.text.include?("Receipt No:") }
```

Set specific time out and message

We can specific maximum wait time (in seconds).

```
Watir::Wait.until(timeout: 10, message: "Timed out for waiting for receipt") {
  browser.text.include?("Receipt No:")
}
```

Here is a sample output when Watir times out on waiting.

```
Watir::Wait::TimeoutError:
timed out after 2 seconds, Timed out for waiting for receipt
# ./spec/ch12_ajax_spec.rb:40:in `block (2 levels) in '
```

If not set, Watir will use the default `Watir.default_timeout`, 30 seconds.

Block code is a condition

`Wait.until{ ... }` waits on a condition to be met. More specifically, a condition if a block of Ruby code returns a boolean value. This won't work if the block code throws an error, typically, unable to find an element, like the example below.

```
Watir::Wait.until{ browser.span(id: "receiptNo").text } # throws error
```

Here is a workaround.

```
Watir::Wait.until{ browser.span(id: "receiptNo"),exists? }
expect(browser.span(id: "receiptNo").text.to_i).to be > 0
```

12.3 Implicit Waits until Time out

An implicit wait is to tell Watir to poll finding a web element (or elements) for a certain amount of time if they are not immediately available. The default setting is 0. Once set, the implicit wait is set for the life of the WebDriver object instance, until its next set.

```
browser.driver.manage.timeouts.implicit_wait = 10 # 10 seconds
browser.button(:value,"Transfer").click
expect(browser.span(id: "receiptNo").text.to_i).to be > 0
browser.driver.manage.timeouts.implicit_wait = 0  # don't wait any more
```

Please note the implicit waits only works on locating elements.

```
browser.driver.manage.timeouts.implicit_wait = 10
browser.button(:value,"Transfer").click
expect(browser.text).to include("Receipt No:") # will fail
```

I would not recommend using Implicit waits as it is easy to forget the reset the implicit value back, and in my opinion, breaks flow of test scripts in terms of readability.

12.4 Wait an object to be present

When testing a dynamic web application, i.e., using AJAX or JavaScript a lot, we need wait a control to be present first before perform actions on it such as clicking or entering texts. Thankfully, Watir provides the following convenient methods:

- object.when_present.do_something
- object.wait_until_present
- object.wait_while_present

Examples:

```
browser.text_field(id: "rcptAmount").when_present.set("250")
browser.button(:value,"Transfer").when_present(2).click
browser.img(:id => "spinner").wait_while_present
browser.span(id: "receiptNo").wait_until_present
expect(browser.label(id: "date").when_present.text).to eq(today)
```

More info can be found at Watir Element Docs[1].

---
[1]http://watir.github.io/watir-webdriver/doc/Watir/Element.html

13. File Upload and Popup dialogs

In this chapter, I will show you how to handle file upload and popup dialogs. Most of pop up dialogs, such as 'Choose File to upload', are native windows rather than browser windows. This would be a challenge for testing as Watir only drives browsers. If one pop up window is not handled properly, test execution will be on halt.

13.1 File upload

Example page

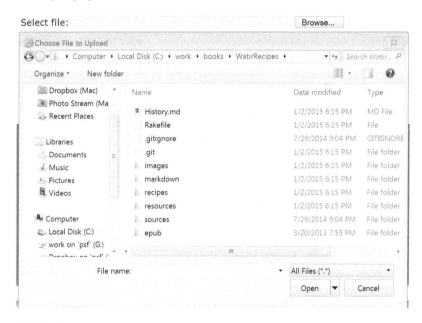

HTML Source

```
<input type="file" name="document[file]" id="files" size="60"/>
```

Test script

```
browser.file_field(name: "document[file]").set("C:\\testdata\\logo.png")
```

The first slash of \\ is for escaping the later one, the whole purpose is to pass the value "C:\testdata\logo.png" to the control.

Some might say, hard coding a file path is not a good practice. Right, it is generally better to include your test data files within your test project, then use relative paths to refer to them:

```
selected_file = File.join(File.dirname(__FILE__), "testdata", "users.csv")
selected_file = selected_file.gsub("/", "\\") if RUBY_PLATFORM =~ /mingw/
browser.file_field(name: "document[file]").set(selected_file)
```

In Ruby, the path separator is '/', the second statement in the above test script is to convert the path using the windows path separator.

13.2 JavaScript pop ups

JavaScript pop ups are created using javascript, commonly used for confirmation or alerting users.

There are many discussions on handling JavaScript Pop ups in Watir forums and Wikis. I tried several approaches. Here I list two:

Handle JavaScript pop ups with JavaScript

```
browser.execute_script "window.confirm = function() { return true; }"
browser.execute_script "window.alert = function() { return true; }"
browser.execute_script "window.prompt = function() { return true; }"
browser.button(:value, " Buy Now ").click
```

This approach works in IE only. (for Watir-WebDriver, use alert API)

This recipe is courtesy of Alister Scott's WatirMelon blog[1]

---

[1]http://watirmelon.com/2010/10/31/dismissing-pesky-javascript-dialogs-with-watir/

13.3 Timeout on an operation

When a pop up window is not handled, it blocks the test execution. It is worse than test failure when running a number of test cases. For operations that are prone to hold ups, we can add a time out.

```
require 'timeout'
Timeout::timeout(5) {
  browser.alert.ok
}
```

13.4 Popup Handler approach

There are other types of pop ups too, such as Basic Authentication and Security warning dialogs. How to handle them? The fundamental difficulty behind pop up dialog handling is that some of these dialogs are native windows, not part of the browser (Watir-Classic drives IE browsers only).

Here I introduce a generic approach to handle all sorts of pop up dialogs. Set up a monitoring process (let's call it popup handler) waiting for notifications of possible new pop ups. Once the popup hander receives one, it will try to handle the pop up dialog with the data received using some kind of technologies to automate native windows. It works like this:

```
# ...
NOTIFY_HANDLER_ABOUT_TO_TRIGGER_A_POPUP_OPERATION
PERFORM_OPERATION
# ...
```

BuildWise Agent is a tool for executing automated tests on multiple machines in parallel. It has a free utility named 'Popup handler' just does that.

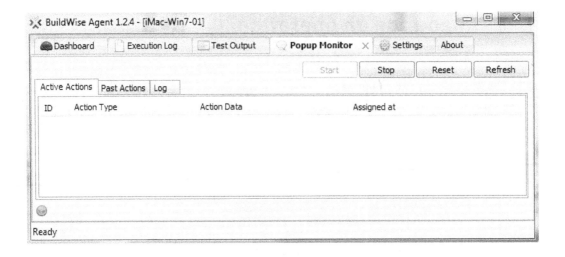

13.5 Handle JavaScript dialog with Popup Handler

```
# this will click 'OK' in popup window
handle_popup(:popup) {
  browser.button(:value, " Buy Now ").click
}
```

The `handle_popup` is a function defined in *popup_handler_helper.rb*, which is included in the same project.

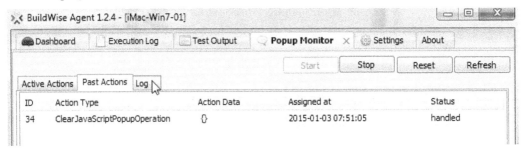

13.6 Basic or Proxy Authentication dialog

```
handle_popup(:basic_auth,
    { :username => "tony",
      :password => "password",
      :win_title => "Windows Security"}) {
  browser.goto("http://itest2.com/svn-demo/")
}
browser.link(text: "tony/").click
```

If Windows XP, change win_title *to "Connect to".*

The same test steps can also be applied to proxy authentication dialogs.

13.7 Internet Explorer modal dialog

Modal dialog, only supported in Internet Explorer, is a dialog (with 'Webpage dialog' suffix in title) that user has to deal with before interacting with the main web page. It is considered as a bad practice, and it is rarely found in modern web sites. However, some unfortunate testers might have to deal with modal dialogs.

Example page

Modal Web Dialogs (only supported in IE)
Show Modal Dialog

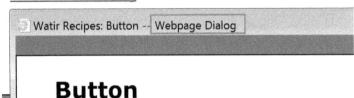

HTML Source

```
<a href="javascript:void(0);" onclick="window.showModalDialog('button.html')">
  Show Modal Dialog</a>
```

Test script (Watir-Classic)

```
main_browser_title = browser.title
browser.link(text, "Show Modal Dialog").click_no_wait
modal_dlg = browser.modal_dialog
expect(modal_dlg.title).to eq("Watir Recipes: Button")
modal_dlg.attach_command
modal_dlg.text_field(name: "user").set("inmodal")
modal_dlg.close

browser = Watir::Browser.attach(:title, main_browser_title)
browser.text_field(name: "status").set("Done")
```

14. Debugging Test Scripts

Debugging usually means analyzing and removing bugs in the code. In the context of automated functional testing, debugging is to find out why a test step did not execute as expected, and then fix it.

14.1 Print text for debugging

```
puts "Now on page: " + browser.title
app_no = browser.label(id: "app_id").text
puts "Application number is " + app_no
```

Here is the output from executing the above test from command line:

```
Now on page: Assertion Test Page
Application number is 1234
```

When the test is executed in a Continuous Integration server, output is normally captured and shown. This can be quite helpful on debugging test execution.

14.2 Write text to IDE output

When developing test scripts in an IDE, it might be convenient to write debugging text to an output window in IDE for easy viewing.

```
puts browser.title
app_no = browser.label(id: "app_id").text
puts "Application number is " + app_no
```

```
it "Write text to TestWise console" do
  debug browser.title
  app_no = browser.label(:id, "app_id").text
  debug "Application number is " + app_no
```

```
Console
Assertion Test Page
Application number is 1234
```

One important matter is that adding this convenience shall not sacrifice the independence of test scripts. That is, the test scripts shall run fine from command line.

14.3 Write page source or element HTML into a file

When the text you want to inspect is large (such as the page source), printing out the text to a console will not be helpful (too much text). A better approach is to write the output to a temporary file and inspect it later. It is often a better way to write to a temporary file, and use some other tool to inspect later.

```
File.open("c:\\temp\\login.html", "w").write(browser.html); # whole page
File.open("c:\\temp\\div_parent.xml", "w").write(browser.div(id: "div_parent").html); # s\
pecific HTML element
```

14.4 Take screenshot

Taking a screenshot of the browser window when an error or failure occurred is a good debugging technique. Watir supports it in a very easy way.

```
browser.screenshot.save("C:\\screenshot.png")
```

The above works. However, when it is run the second time, it will return error "The file already exists". A simple workaround is to write a timestamped file, as below:

```
# save to timestamped file, e.g. screenshot-04071544.png
browser.screenshot.save("C:\\screenshot-#{Time.now.strftime('%m%d%H%M')}.png")
```

Some test IDEs, such as TestWise, has a feature to auto capture screenshots when errors occurred. These screenshots are often included in a test report.

Here is a sample test report containing a screenshot of web page when an error occurred.

14.5 Using IRB

Interactive Ruby (IRB) lets users enter Ruby programs interactively and see the results immediately.

```
> irb
irb(main):001:0> require 'watir'
=> true
irb(main):002:0> browser = Watir::Browser.attach(:index, 0)
=> #<Watir::IE:0x..fc43956e4 url="http://testwisely.com/demo" title="Demo">
irb(main):003:0> browser.link(:text, "NetBank").click
=> 1.09375
```

14.6 Leave browser open after test finishes

Once an error or failure occurred during test execution, a tester's immediate instinct is to check two things: which test statement is failed on and what current web page is like. The first one can be easily found in the testing tools (or command line output). We need the browser to stay open to see the web page. However, we don't want that when running a group of tests, as it will affect the execution of the following test cases.

All of our sample test scripts listed in this book have this:

```
after(:all) do
  browser.close unless debugging?
end
```

That unless debugging? tells TestWise to leave the browser open only when running individual test case. When running multiple test cases, this statement is ignored by TestWise, i.e., the browser will be closed to get ready to run the next test case.

14.7 Pause/Stop test execution at a certain step

Pause, Stop and Run to line are typical debugging features in programming IDEs. If your testing IDE supports them (TestWise Professional edition does, as the screenshot below) and you are comfortable of using them (some are over complicated for debugging test scripts), that's good.

```
browser.select_list(:name, "fromPort").select("New York")
browser.select_list(:id, "departMonth")
browser.select_list(:name, "toPort").se    ▶☰ Run "(Recorded version) Book Flight"
browser.select_list(:id, "returnMonth")    ▶  Run test cases in 'end2end_spec.rb'
browser.select_list(:name, "returnDay")      Run Selected Scripts Against Current Browser
browser.button(:value, "Continue").clic      Run to this line              ▶
```

If not, here I show an extremely simple way: adding a long sleep.

```
#...
sleep 10
#...
```

Once the test execution is on halt, you can do inspection against the web page. Or you can stop the test execution, and use 'attach browser' to retry a certain test statement against the page (see next recipe).

Some may say "This is not good, I don't want to mess up with my test scripts with some sleep statements". It is a fair comment. Back to basics, do what you think appropriate to get the job done.

14.8 Run selected test steps against current browser

In Chapter 8, we covered the recipe for attaching IE browser, a very useful feature for debugging tests. When a test step fails, after analyzing and/or modifying (the test scripts or application), we often would like to rerun the test case continuing from where it stopped, rather than starting from the beginning again.

One solution is to create a temporary test script file with selected test steps, following a test statement to attach current IE window.

```
load File.join(File.dirname(__FILE__), "test_helper.rb")

describe "Debugging" do
  include TestHelper

  it "Run selected test steps" do
    browser = Watir::Browser.attach(:index, 0)
    browser.select_list(id: "returnMonth").select("October 2012")
    browser.select_list(name: "returnDay").select("05")
  end
end
```

It is a good idea to keep this temporary test script file in the same folder as the main test scripts, so that it can keep the references to other dependent files, *test_helper* for example.

The 'Run selected test scripts' feature in TestWise Professional Edition works just this way.

```
40    browser.select_list(:id, "returnMonth").select("October 2012")
41    browser.select_list(:name, "returnDay").select("05")
42    browser.button(:value, "Continue").click
43
44  ⯈ Run "(Recorded version) Book Flight"       Ctrl+Shift+F10      et "Bob"
45  ⯈ Run test cases in 'end2end_spec.rb'        Shift+F10           t "Builder"
46    Run Selected Scripts Against Current Browser
```

15. Test Data

Gathering test data is an important but often neglected activity. Thanks to the power and flexibility of Ruby, testers now have a new ability to prepare test data.

15.1 Get date dynamically

```
require 'date' # only need to require once
# assume today is 2014-10-25
Date.today.strftime("%m/%d/%Y")  # => 03/25/2014
(Time.now + 1 * 24 * 3600).strftime("%Y-%m-%d %H:%M") => # 2014-03-26 12:24
```

Based on the above, we can create easy to read date related functions (see the helper method in the sample project), like the one below

```
# default to UK/AUS date format
def today(date_format = "%d/%m/%Y")
  date_format = "%m/%d/%Y" if date_format.to_s == "us"
  Date.today.strftime(date_format)
end
```

Then you can use the following in your test scripts.

```
today               #=> 25/10/2014
today(:us)          #=> 10/26/2014
today("%Y-%m-%d")   #=> 2014-10-26
```

rwebspec_utils.rb (included in recipe source zip file, available on the book site[1]) contains a set of date related helper methods:

---

[1]http://zhimin.com/books/watir-recipes

```
yesterday            # 24/10/2014
tomorrow             # 26/10/2014
days_from_now(3)     # 29/10/2014
days_before(3)       # 23/10/2014
```

Example use

```
expect(label(id: "date")).to eq(today)
```

15.2 Get a random boolean value

A boolean value means either *true* or *false*. Getting a random true or false might not sound that interesting. That was what I thought when I first learned it. Later, I realized that it is actually very powerful, because I can fill the computer program (test script as well) with nondeterministic data.

```
rand(2) == 1 # true or false
```

For example, in a user sign up form, we could write two cases: one for male and one for female. With random boolean, I could achieve the same with just one test case. If the test case get run many times, it will cover both scenarios.

```
browser.radio(:name => "gender", :value => (rand(2) == 1 ? "male" : "female") ).click
```

15.3 Generate a number within a range

```
rand(10) # a random number 0 up to 9, different each run
rand(90) + 10 # a number between 10 and 99
```

The test statement below will enter a number between 16 to 96. If the test gets run hundreds of times, not a problem at all for an automated test, it will cover driver's input for all permitted ages.

```
browser.text_field(id: "drivers_age").set(random(80) + 16)
```

15.4 Get a random character

```
# the random_number() method is defined in rwebspec_utils.rb in book source
random_number(97, 122).chr # lower case, a..z
random_number(65, 90).chr  # up case, A..Z
```

15.5 Get a random string at fixed length

```
# generate 10 characters lower case string
10.times.inject([]) { |str, el| str << random_number(97, 122).chr }.join
```

The above statement is quite complex. By creating some utility functions (you can find in source project), we can get quite readable test scripts as below:

```
puts random_str(7) #  example: "dolorem"
puts words(5) #  example: "sit doloremque consequatur accusantium aut"
puts sentences(3)
puts paragraphs(2)
```

15.6 Get a random string in a collection

```
random_string_in(["Yes", "No", "Maybe"]  # one of these strings
```

I frequently use this in my test scripts.

15.7 Generate random person names, emails, addresses with Faker

Faker[2] is a Ruby library that generates fake data.

---

[2]https://github.com/stympy/faker

```
require 'faker'
Faker::Name.name              # => "Jeromy Erdman"
Faker::Internet.email         # => "justine_wolf@ryan.com"
Faker::Address.street_address # => "290 Nienow Flats"
Faker::PhoneNumber.phone_number # => "(206)223-6173"
```

You can find more examples at Faker[3] web site. By default, addresses and phone numbers are US format, however, you can switch to another locale or add customization[4].

15.8 Generate a test file at fixed sizes

When testing file uploads, testers often try test files in different sizes. The following ruby statement generates a test file in precise size on the fly.

```
File.open(File.join(File.dirname(__FILE__), "tmp", "2MB.txt"), "w") {|f|
  f.write( '0' * 1024 * 1024 * 2 )
}
```

15.9 Retrieve data from Database

The ultimate way to obtain accurate test data is to retrieve from the database. For many projects, this might not be possible. For ones do, this provides flexibility in terms of getting test data.

The test script example below is to enter the oldest (by age) user's login into the text field on a web page. To get this oldest user in the system, I use SQL to query the database directly (SQLite3 in this example, it will be different for yours, but the concept is the same).

---

[3]https://github.com/stympy/faker
[4]https://github.com/stympy/faker#customization

```ruby
require 'sqlite3'
db = SQLite3::Database.new File.join(File.dirname(__FILE__), "testdata", "sample.db")

# Users table: with login, name, age
oldest_user_login = nil
db.execute( "select * from users order by age desc" ) do |row|
  oldest_user_login = row[0]
  break
end

puts oldest_user_login
browser.goto(site_url.gsub("index.html", "text_field.html"))
browser.text_field(id: "user").set(oldest_user_login)
```

16. Browser Profile and Capabilities

Watir *(not classic)* can start browser instances with various profile preferences which can be quite useful. Obviously, some preference settings are browser specific, so you might take some time to explore. In this chapter, I will cover some common usage.

16.1 Get browser type and version

Detecting browser type and version is useful to write custom test scripts for different browsers.

```
browser = Watir::Browser.new(:firefox)
browser_name = browser.driver.browser
puts browser_name # firefox

puts browser.driver.browser # => firefox
puts browser.driver.capabilities.platform # => mac
puts browser.driver.capabilities.version # => 72.0.1

expect(browser.driver.browser).to eq(:firefox)
if RUBY_PLATFORM =~ /darwin/
  if browser_name.to_s == "firefox"
    expect(browser.driver.capabilities.platform).to eq("mac")
  else
    expect(browser.driver.capabilities.platform).to eq("mac os x")
  end
elsif RUBY_PLATFORM =~ /mingw/
  # old versions return :winnt
  expect(browser.driver.capabilities.platform).to eq(:windows)
end
```

16.2 Set HTTP Proxy for Browser

Here is an example to set HTTP proxy server for Firefox browser.

```
profile = Selenium::WebDriver::Firefox::Profile.new
profile['network.proxy.type'] = 1
# http://kb.mozillazine.org/Network.proxy.type

profile['network.proxy.http'] = "myproxy.com"
profile['network.proxy.http_port'] = 3128
browser = Watir::Browser.new(:firefox,  options: {profile: profile})
browser.goto "http://testwisely.com/demo"
```

16.3 Verify file download in Chrome

To efficiently verify a file is downloaded, we would like to

- save the file to a specific folder
- avoid "Open with or Save File" dialog

```
# Change default download directory. On Mac, default to /Users/YOU/Downloads folder
download_path = RUBY_PLATFORM =~ /mingw/ ? "C:\\TEMP" : "/Users/zhimin/tmp"
prefs = {
  :download => {
    :prompt_for_download => false,
    :default_directory => download_path,
  },
}
browser = Watir::Browser.new(:chrome, options: { prefs: prefs })
browser.goto "http://zhimin.com/books/pwta"
browser.link(:text => "Download").click
# wait download to complete
Watir::Wait.until(timeout: 20) {
  File.exists?("#{download_path}/practical-web-test-automation-sample.pdf")
}
```

This is the new way (from v2.37) to pass preferences to Chrome. More Chrome preferences: http://src.chromium.org/svn/trunk/src/chrome/common/pref_names.cc[1]

16.4 Test downloading PDF in Firefox

---

[1]http://src.chromium.org/svn/trunk/src/chrome/common/pref_names.cc

```
download_path = RUBY_PLATFORM =~ /mingw/ ? "C:\\TEMP": "/Users/zhimin/tmp"
profile = Selenium::WebDriver::Firefox::Profile.new
profile["browser.download.folderList"] = 2
profile["browser.download.dir"] = download_path
profile["browser.helperApps.neverAsk.saveToDisk"] = 'application/pdf'
# disable Firefox's built-in PDF viewer
profile["pdfjs.disabled"] = true

browser = Watir::Browser.new(:firefox,  options: {profile: profile})
browser.goto "http://zhimin.com/books/selenium-recipes"
browser.link(:text => "Download").click
Watir::Wait.until(timeout: 20) {
  File.exists?("#{download_path}/selenium-recipes-in-ruby-sample.pdf")
}
```

16.5 Start Firefox with extension

Make sure you download the extension file (.xpi) first.

```
profile = Selenium::WebDriver::Firefox::Profile.new
ext_path = File.join(File.dirname(__FILE__), "..",
 "read_aloud_a_text_to_speech_voice_reader-1.48.0-an+fx.xpi")
@browser = Watir::Browser.new(:firefox, options: { profile: profile })
@browser.driver.install_addon(ext_path)
@browser.goto("https://whenwise.agileway.net")
sleep 3 # shall see extension icon
```

Please note the 'installed' extension is only for the test Firefox session, won't affect the
default Firefox profile.

16.6 Manage Cookies

```
browser = Watir::Browser.new(:firefox)
browser.goto("http://travel.agileway.net")
browser.driver.manage.add_cookie(:name => "username", :value => "natalie" )
browser.driver.manage.all_cookies.each do |a_cookie|
  # puts a_cookie.inspect
end
puts browser.driver.manage.cookie_named("username")[:value] # => "natalie"
```

16.7 Headless Chrome

Chrome 59 (released on June 5, 2017) introduces headless mode, which can be used with Watir. Here is how:

```
browser = Watir::Browser.new(:chrome, :headless => true)
browser.goto("https://whenwise.agileway.net")
expect(browser.title).to eq("WhenWise - Booking Made Easy")
```

Be aware of headless browser simulation in test automation

Between 2010–2015, Headless browser testing with PhantomJS was hyped highly by test architects/engineers. I had my doubts on this headless testing with browser simulation for the reasons below:

- It is NOT a real browser.
- I need to inspect the web page when a test failed, I cannot do that with PhantomJS. In test automation, as we know, we perform this all the time.
- To achieve faster execution time, I prefer distributing tests to multiple build agents to rum them in parallel as a part of the Continuous Testing process. That way, I get not only much faster execution time (throwing in more machines), also get useful features such as quick feedback, rerunning failed tests on another build agent, dynamic execution ordering by priority, etc. All in real browsers.

On April 13, 2017: PhantomJS was deprecated[a].

---
[a]https://groups.google.com/forum/m/#!topic/phantomjs/9aI5d-LDuNE

16.8 Test responsive websites

Modern websites embrace responsive design to fit in different screen resolutions on various devices, such as iPad and smartphones. Bootstrap is a very popular responsive framework. How to verify your web site's responsiveness is a big question, it depends what you want to test. A quick answer is to use WebDriver's `driver.manage().window().resize_to` to set your browser to a target resolution, and then execute tests.

The example below verify a text box's width changes when switching from a desktop computer to a iPad, basically, whether responsive is enabled or not..

```
browser = Watir::Browser.new(browser_type)
browser.window.resize_to(1024, 768) # Desktop
browser.goto("https://agileway.net")
width_desktop = browser.text_field(name: "email").wd.size.width # webdriver used here
puts(width_desktop)
browser.window.resize_to(768, 1024) # iPad
width_ipad = browser.text_field(name: "email").wd.size.width
puts(width_ipad)
expect(width_desktop).to be < width_ipad    # 358 vs 960
```

17. Advanced User Interactions

The ActionBuilder in Selenium WebDriver provides a way to set up and perform complex user interactions. Specifically, grouping a series of keyboard and mouse operations and sending to the browser.

Mouse interactions

- click
- click_and_hold
- context_click
- double_click
- drag_and_drop
- drag_and_drop_by
- move_by
- move_to
- release

Keyboard interactions

- key_down
- key_up
- send_keys

The usage

You may use the above ActionBuilder operations in Watir via 'driver'.

`browser.driver.action.` + one or more above operations + `.perform`

Watir provides several convenient wrapper methods, such as `double_click`, `drag_and_drop`, ..., etc.

17.1 Double click a control

```
browser.goto(site_url + "/text_field.html")
quick_fill_elem = browser.span(id: "quickfill")
quick_fill_elem.double_click    # double click to fill
```

Under the hood, Watir uses Selenium's ActionBuilder
`driver.action.double_click(@element).perform`. You may invoke ActionBuilder directly in Watir.

```
browser.driver.action.double_click(browser.span(id: "quickfill").wd).perform
```

It is important to note that before using ActionBuilder, we need to convert the Watir element to Selenium's, that is, `elem.wd`.

17.2 Move mouse to a control - Mouse Over

```
elem = browser.element(id: "email")
elem.hover
```

The equivalent in ActionBuilder:

```
browser.driver.action.move_to(elem.wd).perform
```

17.3 Click and hold - select multiple items

The test scripts below click and hold to select three controls in a grid.

```
browser.goto("http://jqueryui.com/selectable")
browser.link(:text, "Display as grid").click
sleep 0.5
list_items = browser.iframe(:index => 0).lis(xpath: "//ol[@id='selectable']/li")
browser.driver.action.click_and_hold(list_items[1].wd).click_and_hold(list_items[3].wd).c\
lick.perform
browser.link(:text, "view source").click # on main content page
```

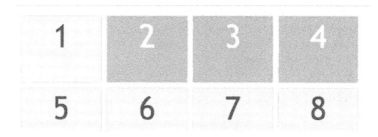

17.4 Context Click - right click a control

```
browser.goto(site_url + "/text_field.html")
sleep 0.5
browser.text_field(id: "pass").right_click
```

The below is a browser specific test to click "Paste" on the context menu in Firefox.

```
if browser.driver.capabilities.browser_name == "firefox"
  elem = browser.element(id: "pass")
  browser.driver.action.context_click(elem.wd).
    send_keys(:down).send_keys(:down).
    send_keys(:down).send_keys(:down).
    send_keys(:return).perform
end
```

17.5 Drag and drop

Drag-n-drop is increasingly common in new web sites. Testing this feature can be largely achieved in Watir WebDriver, I used the word 'largely' which means achieving the same outcome, but not the 'mouse dragging' part. In this example page,

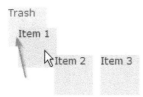

the test script below will *drop* 'Item 1' to 'Trash'.

```
browser.goto(site_url + "/drag_n_drop.html")
drag_from = browser.element(id: "item_1")
target = browser.element(id: "trash")
drag_from.drag_and_drop_on(target)
```

The below is a screenshot after the test execution.

17.6 Drag slider

Slider (a part of JQuery UI library) provide users an very intuitive way to adjust values (typically in settings).

Slider

The test below simulates 'dragging the slider to the right'.

```
browser.goto(site_url + "/html5.html")
expect(browser.div(id: "pass_rate").text).to eq("15%")
elem = browser.element(id: "pass-rate-slider")
elem.drag_and_drop_by(2, 0) # unable to set specific value
expect(browser.element(id: "pass_rate").text).not_to eq("15%")
```

More information about `drag_and_drop_by` can be found at Selenium ActionBuild Ruby API[1].

The below is a screenshot after the test execution.

Slider

---

[1]http://selenium.googlecode.com/git/docs/api/rb/Selenium/WebDriver/ActionBuilder.html#drag_and_drop_by-instance_method

Please note that the percentage figure after executing the test above are always 50% (I saw 49% now and then).

17.7 Send key sequences - Select All and Delete

```
browser.goto(site_url + "/text_field.html")
browser.textarea(id: "comments").send_keys("Multiple Line\r\n Text")
elem = browser.element(id: "comments")
browser.driver.action.click(elem.wd).
  key_down(:control).
  send_keys("a").
  key_up(:control).
  perform

# this different from click element, the key is send to browser directly
browser.send_keys(:backspace)
```

Please note that the last test statement is different from elem.send_keys. The keystrokes triggered by browser.send_keys is sent to the active element in the browser window.

18. HTML 5 and JavaScript

Web technologies are evolving. HTML5 includes many new features for more dynamic web applications and interfaces. Furthermore, wide use of JavaScript (thanks to popular JavaScript libraries such as JQuery), web sites nowadays are much more dynamic. In this chapter, I will show some Selenium examples to test HTML5 elements and interactive operations with JavaScript.

Please note that some tests only work on certain browsers (Chrome is your best bet), as some HTML5 features are not fully supported in some browsers yet.

18.1 HTML5 Email type field

Let's start with a simple one. An email type field is used for input fields that should contain an e-mail address. From the testing point of view, we treat it exactly the same as a normal text field.

Email field

> jam

HTML Source

```
<input id="email" name="email" type="email" style="height:30px; width: 280px;">
```

```
browser.text_field(id: "email").send_keys("test@wisely.com")
```

18.2 HTML5 Time Field

The HTML5 time field is much more complex, as you can see from the screenshot below. *Please note that, at the time of writing, only Chrome support this time field.*

Time

08:27 AM ✕ ⏶⏷

HTML Source

```
<input id="start_time_1" name="start_time" type="time" style="height:30px; width: 120px;">
```

Watir does support Time field directly.

```
browser.text_field(id: "start_time_1").send_keys("12:05AM") # error
```

The above test statement will return an error.

```
unable to locate element, using {:id=>"start_time_1", :tag_name=>"input or textarea", :ty\
pe=>"(any text type)"}
```

However, we can achieve testing this by using Selenium WebDriver directly.

```
browser.driver.find_element(id: "start_time_1").send_keys("12:05AM")
```

This test statement only works with a recent ChromeDriver, previously, I have to do these:

1. make sure the focus is not on this time field control
2. click and focus the time field
3. clear existing time
4. enter a new time

```
# focus on another ...
browser.driver.find_element(id: "home_link").send_keys("")
sleep 0.5

# now back to change it
browser.driver.find_element(id: "start_time_1").click
browser.driver.find_element(id: "start_time_1").send_keys([:delete, :left, :delete, :left\
, :delete])

browser.driver.find_element(id: "start_time_1").send_keys("08")
sleep 0.3
browser.driver.find_element(id: "start_time_1").send_keys("27")
sleep 0.3
browser.driver.find_element(id: "start_time_1").send_keys("AM")
```

18.3 Invoke 'onclick' JavaScript event

In the example below, when user clicks on the text field control, the tip text (*'Max 20 characters'*) is shown.

Example page

Max 20 characters

HTML Source

```
<input type="text" name="person_name" onclick="$('#tip').show();" onchange="change_perso\
n_name(this.value);"/>
<span id="tip" style="display:none; margin-left: 20px; color:gray;">Max 20 characters</sp\
an>
```

When we use normal set in Watir, it enters the text OK, but the tip text is not displayed.

```
browser.text_field(name:  "person_name").set "Wise Tester"
```

We can simply call 'click' to achieve it.

```
browser.text_field(name:  "person_name").click
# OR
# browser.text_field(name:  "person_name").fire_event("onclick")
expect(browser.span(id: "tip").text).to eq("Max 20 characters")
```

18.4 Invoke JavaScript events such as 'onchange'

A generic way to invoke 'OnXXXX' events is to execute JavaScript, the below is an example
to invoke 'OnChange' event on a text box.

```
browser.goto( site_url +  "/select_list.html")
browser.text_field(id: "person_name_textbox").set "Test Wise"
browser.execute_script("$('#person_name_textbox').trigger('change')");
# OR
# browser.execute_script("return document.getElementById('person_name_textbox').fireEvent\
('OnChange')");
expect(browser.label(id: "person_name_label").text).to eq("Test Wise")
```

18.5 Chosen - Standard Select

Chosen is a popular JQuery plug-in that makes long select lists more user-friendly, it turns
the standard HTML select list box into this:

HTML Source

```
<select id="chosen_single" class="chosen-select"  data-placeholder="Choose a Country..." \
style="width:350px;">
  <option value=""></option>
  <option value="United States">United States</option>
  <option value="United Kingdom">United Kingdom</option>
  <option value="Australia">Australia</option>
</select>
```

The HTML source seems not much different from the standard select list excepting adding the class chosen-select. By using the class as the identification, the JavaScript included on the page generates the following HTML fragment (beneath the select element).

Generated HTML Source

```
<div class="chosen-container chosen-container-single chosen-container-active" style="widt\
h: 350px;" title="" id="chosen_single_chosen">
  <a class="chosen-single chosen-default" tabindex="-1"><span>Choose a Country...</span><\
div><b></b></div></a>
  <div class="chosen-drop">
    <div class="chosen-search">
      <input type="text" autocomplete="off" tabindex="2">
    </div>
    <ul class="chosen-results">
      <li class="active-result" style="" data-option-array-index="1">United States</li>
      <li class="active-result result-selected" style="" data-option-array-index="2">Unit\
ed Kingdom</li>
      <li class="active-result" style="" data-option-array-index="3">Australia</li>
    </ul>
  </div>
</div>
```

Please note that this dynamically generated HTML fragment is not viewable by 'View Page Source', you need to enable the inspection tool (usually right mouse click the page, then choose 'Inspect Element') to see it.

Before we test it, we need to understand how we use it.

- Click the 'Choose a Country'
- Select an option

There is no difference from the standard select list. That's correct, we need to understand how Chosen emulates the standard select list first. In Chosen, clicking the 'Choose a Country' is actually clicking a hyper link with class "chosen-single" under the div with ID "chosen_-single_chosen" (the ID is whatever set in the select element, followed by '_chosen'); selecting an option is clicking an list item (tag: li) with class 'active-result'. With that knowledge, plus XPath in Selenium, we can drive a Chosen standard select box with the test scripts below:

```
browser.goto( site_url + "/chosen/index.html")
sleep 2 # wait enough time to load JS
browser.link(xpath:  "//div[@id='chosen_single_chosen']//a[contains(@class,'chosen-single\
')]").click
available_items = browser.lis(xpath:  "//div[@id='chosen_single_chosen']//div[@class='cho\
sen-drop']//li[contains(@class,'active-result')]")
available_items.select{|x| x.text == "Australia"}.first.click

sleep 1
browser.link(xpath:  "//div[@id='chosen_single_chosen']//a[contains(@class,'chosen-single\
')]").click
available_items = browser.lis(xpath:  "//div[@id='chosen_single_chosen']//div[@class='cho\
sen-drop']//li[contains(@class,'active-result')]")
available_items.select{|x| x.text == "United States"}.first.click
```

A neat feature of Chosen is allowing user to search the option list, to do that in Watir:

```
sleep 1
browser.link(xpath:  "//div[@id='chosen_single_chosen']//a[contains(@class,'chosen-single\
')]").click

search_text_field = browser.text_field(xpath:  "//div[@id='chosen_single_chosen']//div[@c\
lass='chosen-drop']//div[contains(@class,'chosen-search')]/input")
search_text_field.send_keys("United King")
sleep 0.5 # let filtering finishing
# select first selected option
search_text_field.send_keys(:enter)
```

18.6 Chosen - Multiple Select

Chosen[1] also enhances the multiple selection (a lot).

---
[1]http://harvesthq.github.io/chosen/

HTML Source

```
<select id="chosen_multiple" class="chosen-select" multiple data-placeholder="Choose a Co\
untry..."  style="width:350px;">
  <option value=""></option>
  <option value="United States">United States</option>
  <option value="United Kingdom">United Kingdom</option>
  <option value="Australia">Australia</option>
</select>
```

Again, the only difference from the standard multiple select list is the class 'chosen-select'.

Generated HTML Source

```
<div class="chosen-container chosen-container-multi chosen-container-active" style="width\
: 350px;" title="" id="chosen_multiple_chosen">
  <ul class="chosen-choices">
    <li class="search-choice"><span>Australia</span><a class="search-choice-close" data-o\
ption-array-index="3"></a></li>
    <li class="search-choice"><span>United States</span><a class="search-choice-close" da\
ta-option-array-index="1"></a></li>
    <li class="search-field"><input type="text" value="Choose a Country..." class="" auto\
complete="off" style="width: 25px;" tabindex="4"></li>
  </ul>
  <div class="chosen-drop">
    <ul class="chosen-results">
      <li class="result-selected" style="" data-option-array-index="1">United States</li>
      <li class="active-result" style="" data-option-array-index="2">United Kingdom</li>
      <li class="result-selected" style="" data-option-array-index="3">Australia</li>
      </ul>
  </div>
</div>
```

Astute readers will find the generated HTML fragment is quite different from the standard (single) select, that's because of the usage. The concept of working out driving the control is the same, I will leave the homework to you, just show the test scripts.

```
sleep 2 # wait the JS to load fully
# click the box then select one option
browser.text_field(xpath:  "//div[@id='chosen_multiple_chosen']//li[@class='search-field'\
]/input").click
available_items = browser.lis(xpath:  "//div[@id='chosen_multiple_chosen']//div[@class='c\
hosen-drop']//li[contains(@class,'active-result')]")
available_items.select{|x| x.text == "Australia"}.first.click

# select another
browser.text_field(xpath:  "//div[@id='chosen_multiple_chosen']//li[@class='search-field'\
]/input").click
available_items = browser.lis(xpath:  "//div[@id='chosen_multiple_chosen']//div[@class='c\
hosen-drop']//li[contains(@class,'active-result')]")
available_items.select{|x| x.text == "United Kingdom"}.first.click
```

To deselect an option is to click the little 'x' on the right. In fact, it is the idea to clear all selections first then select the wanted options.

```
# clear all selections
sleep 0.5
close_btns = browser.links(xpath:  "//div[@id='chosen_multiple_chosen']//ul[@class='chose\
n-choices']/li[contains(@class,'search-choice')]/a[contains(@class,'search-choice-close')\
]")
close_btns.each do |cb|
  cb.click
end

browser.text_field(xpath:  "//div[@id='chosen_multiple_chosen']//li[@class='search-field'\
]/input").click
available_items = browser.lis(xpath:  "//div[@id='chosen_multiple_chosen']//div[@class='c\
hosen-drop']//li[contains(@class,'active-result')]")
available_items.select{|x| x.text == "United States"}.first.click
```

Some might say the test scripts are quite complex. That's good thinking, if many of our test steps are written like this, it will be quite hard to maintain. One common way is to extract them into reusable functions, like below:

```
def clear_chosen(chosen_select_id)
  sleep 0.5
  close_btns = browser.links(xpath:  "//div[@id='#{chosen_select_id}']//ul[@class='chosen\
-choices']/li[contains(@class,'search-choice')]/a[contains(@class,'search-choice-close')]\
")
  close_btns.each do |cb|
    cb.click
  end
end


def select_chosen_label(chosen_select_id, option_label)
  browser.text_field(xpath:  "//div[@id='#{chosen_select_id}']//li[@class='search-field']\
/input").click
  available_items = browser.lis(xpath:  "//div[@id='#{chosen_select_id}']//div[@class='ch\
osen-drop']//li[contains(@class,'active-result')]")
  available_items.select{|x| x.text == option_label}.first.click
end

# ...

it "Wrap chosen in reusable functions" do
  # ... land to the page with a chosen select list
  sleep 1

  clear_chosen("chosen_multiple_chosen")
  select_chosen_label("chosen_multiple_chosen", "United States")
  select_chosen_label("chosen_multiple_chosen", "Australia")
end
```

You can find more techniques for writing maintainable tests from my other book *Practical Web Test Automation*[2].

18.7 AngularJS web pages

AngularJS is a popular client-side JavaScript framework that can be used to extend HTML. Here is a web page (simple TODO list) developed in AngularJS.

---

[2]https://leanpub.com/practical-web-test-automation

1 of 2 remaining [archive]

- ☑ ~~learn angular~~
- ☐ build an angular app

| add new todo here | add |

HTML Source

The page source (via "View Page Source" in browser) is different from what you saw on the page. It contains some kind of dynamic coding (*ng-xxx*).

```
<div ng-controller="TodoCtrl">
  <span>{{remaining()}} of {{todos.length}} remaining</span>
  [ <a href="" ng-click="archive()">archive</a> ]
  <ul class="unstyled">
    <li ng-repeat="todo in todos">
      <input type="checkbox" ng-model="todo.done">
      <span class="done-{{todo.done}}">{{todo.text}}</span>
    </li>
  </ul>
  <form ng-submit="addTodo()">
    <input type="text" ng-model="todoText"  size="30"
           placeholder="add new todo here">
    <input class="btn-primary" type="submit" value="add">
  </form>
</div>
```

As a tester, we don't need to worry about AngularJS programming logic in the page source. To view rendered page source, which matters for testing, inspect the page via right mouse click page and select "Inspect Element".

Browser inspect view

Astute readers will notice that the 'name' attribute are missing in the input elements, replaced with 'ng-model' instead. We can use xpath to identify the web element.

The tests script below

- Add a new todo item in a text field
- Click add button
- Uncheck the 3rd todo item

```
expect(browser.html).to include("1 of 2 remaining")
browser.text_field(xpath:  "//input[@ng-model='todoText']").set("Learn test automation")
browser.button(:value, "add").click
sleep 0.5
browser.checkboxes(xpath:  "//input[@type = 'checkbox' and @ng-model='todo.done']")[2].cl\
ick
sleep 1
expect(browser.html).to include("1 of 3 remaining")
```

18.8 Ember JS web pages

Ember JS is another JavaScript web framework, like Angular JS, the 'Page Source' view (from browser) of a web page is raw source code, which is not useful for testing.

HTML Source

```
<div class="control-group">
  <label class="control-label" for="longitude">Longitude</label>
  <div class="controls">
    {{view Ember.TextField valueBinding="longitude"}}
  </div>
</div>
```

Browser inspect view

```
  <label class="control-label" for="longitude">
      Longitude
  </label>
  <div class="controls">
    <input id="ember412" class="ember-view ember-text-field" type="text"></input>
  </div>
```

The ID attribute of a Ember JS generated element (by default) changes. For example, this text field ID is "ember412".

Refresh the page, the ID changed to a different value.

So we shall use another way to identify the element.

```
browser.goto(site_url + "/emberjs-crud-rest/index.html")
browser.link(:text, "Locations").click
browser.link(:text, "New location").click

ember_text_fields = browser.text_fields(xpath:  "//div[@class='controls']/input[@class='e\
mber-view ember-text-field']")
ember_text_fields[0].set("-24.0034583945")
ember_text_fields[1].set("146.903459345")
ember_text_fields[2].set("90%")

browser.button(:value, "Update record").click
```

18.9 "Share Location" with Firefox

HTML5 Geolocation API can obtain a user's position. By using Geolocation API, programmers can develop web applications to provide location-aware services, such as locating the nearest restaurants. When a web page wants to use a user's location information, the user is presented with a pop up for permission.

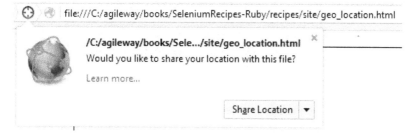

This is a native popup window, which means Selenium WebDriver cannot drive it. However, there is a workaround. We can set up a browser profile that pre-allows "Share Location" for specific websites. Here are the steps for Firefox.

1. Open Firefox with a specific profile for testing
2. Open the site
3. Type about:permissions in the address
4. Select the site and choose "Allow" option for "Share Location"

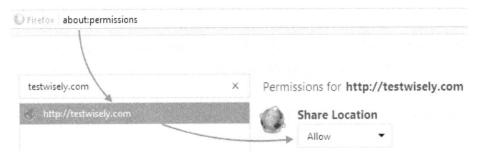

The set up and use of a specific testing profile for Firefox is already covered in Chapter 16. This only needs to be done once. After that, the test script can test location-aware web pages.

```
profile = Selenium::WebDriver::Firefox::Profile.from_name 'testing'
@browser = Watir::Browser.new(:firefox, :profile => profile)
@browser.goto("http://testwisely.com/demo/geo-location")
browser.button(id: "use_current_location_btn").click
Watir::Wait.until {browser.p(id: "demo").text.include?("Latitude:") }
```

18.10 Faking Geolocation with JavaScript

With Geolocation testing, it is almost certain that we will need to test the users in different locations. This can be done by JavaScript.

```
lati = -34.915379
longti = 138.576777
browser.execute_script("window.navigator.geolocation.getCurrentPosition=function(success)\
{; var position = {'coords' : {'latitude': '#{lati}','longitude': '#{longti}'}}; success\
(position);}");
browser.button(id: "use_current_location_btn").click
try_for(10) { expect(browser.p(id: "demo").text).to include("-34.915379")  }
```

19. WYSIWYG HTML editors

WYSIWYG (an acronym for "What You See Is What You Get") HTML editors are widely used in web applications as embedded text editor nowadays. In this chapter, we will use Watir to test several popular WYSIWYG HTML editors.

19.1 TinyMCE

TinyMCE is a web-based WYSIWYG editor, it claims "the most used WYSIWYG editor in the world, it is used by millions"[1].

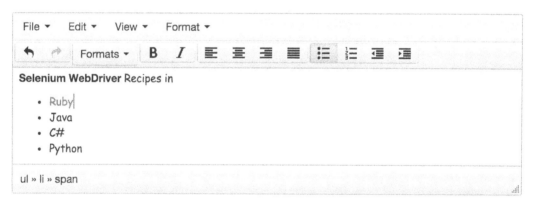

The rich text is rendered inside an inline frame within TinyMCE. To test it, we need to "switch to" that frame.

---

[1]http://www.tinymce.com/enterprise/using.php

```
browser.goto(site_url + "/tinymce-4.1.9/tinyice_demo.html")
sleep 1 # wait JavaScript to load

editor_body = browser.iframe(id: 'mce_0_ifr').body(id: 'tinymce')
# Populate editor content with HTML directly
browser.iframe(id: 'mce_0_ifr').execute_script("arguments[0].innerHTML = '<h1>Heading</h1\
>AgileWay'", editor_body)
sleep 1

editor_body.send_keys("New content") # 'Typing' text
sleep 1
editor_body.wd.clear

browser.execute_script("arguments[0].innerHTML = '<p>one</p><p>two</p>'", editor_body)

# drive controls on the main page, click TinyMCE editor's 'Numbered List' button
browser.button(xpath: "//div[@aria-label='Numbered list']/button").click

# Insert text calling JavaScript
browser.execute_script("tinyMCE.activeEditor.insertContent('<p>Brisbane</p>')")
```

19.2 CKEditor

CKEditor is another popular WYSIWYG editor. Like TinyMCE, CKEditor uses an inline frame.

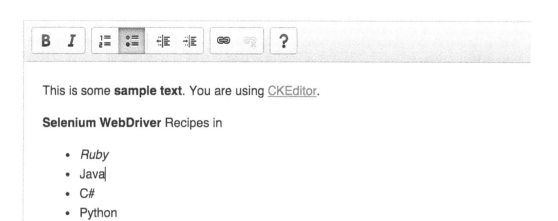

```
browser.goto(site_url + "/ckeditor-4.4.7/samples/uicolor.html")
sleep 1 # wait JS to load
editor_body = browser.iframe(index: 0).body
editor_body.send_keys("Watir Recipes\n by Zhimin Zhan")
sleep 1

# Clear content Another Method Using ActionBuilder to clear()
browser.driver.action.click(editor_body.wd).key_down(:control).send_keys("a").key_up(:con\
trol).perform
browser.driver.action.send_keys(:backspace).perform

browser.link(class: "cke_button__numberedlist").click() # numbered list
editor_body.send_keys("ClinicWise")
editor_body.send_keys(:enter)
```

19.3 SummerNote

SummerNote is a Bootstrap based lightweight WYSIWYG editor, different from TinyMCE or CKEditor, it does not use frames.

Selenium WebDriver Recipes in

- Ruby
- Java
- C#
- Python

```
browser.goto(site_url + "/summernote-0.6.3/demo.html")
sleep 0.5
browser.div(:class => 'note-editor').div(class: 'note-editable').send_keys("Text")
# click a format button: unordered list
browser.button(xpath: "//button[@data-event='insertUnorderedList']").click
# switch to code view
browser.button(xpath: "//button[@data-event='codeview']").click()
# insert text to code editor, calling .set("") will replace text
browser.textarea(xpath: "//textarea[@class='note-codable']").send_keys("\n<p>HTML</p>")
```

19.4 CodeMirror

CodeMirror is a versatile text editor implemented in JavaScript. CodeMirror is not a
WYSIWYG editor, but it is often used with one for editing raw HTML source for the rich
text content.

```
1 <!-- write some xml below -->
2 <Selenium-WebDriverRecipes>
3   <book>in Ruby</book>
4   <book>in Java</book>
5   <book>in C#</book>
6   <book>in Python</book>
7 </
      </Selenium-WebDriverRecipes>
```

```
browser.goto(site_url + "/codemirror-5.1/demo/xmlcomplete.html")
elem = browser.element(class: "CodeMirror-scroll")
elem.click
sleep 0.5
# elem.send_keys does not work
browser.send_keys("<A>")
```

20. Leverage Programming

The reason that WebDriver quickly overtakes other commercial testing tools (typically promoting record-n-playback), in my opinion, is embracing the programming, which offers the flexibility needed for maintainable automated test scripts.

In the chapter, I will show some examples that use some programming practices to help our testing needs.

20.1 Raise exceptions to fail test

While RSpec Expectation or MiniTest framework provides most of assertions needed, raising exceptions can be useful too as shown below.

```
raise "Unsupported platform #{RUBY_PLATFORM}" unless RUBY_PLATFORM.include?("darwin")
```

In test output (when running on Windows):

```
Unsupported platform i386-mingw32
# ./spec/ch20_programming_spec.rb: ...
```

An exception means an anomalous or exceptional condition occurred. The code to handle exceptions is called exception handling, an important concept in programming. If an exception is not handled, the program execution will terminate with the exception displayed.

Here is anther more complete example.

```
begin
  driver = Selenium::WebDriver.for(:chrome)
  # ...
rescue => e
  puts "Exception occurred: #{e}, #{e.backtrace}"
ensure
  driver.quit
end
```

`rescue` block handles the exception. If an exception is handled, the program (in our case, test execution) continues. `e.backtrace` returns the stack trace of the exception occurred. `ensure` block is always run (after) no matter exceptions are thrown (from `begin`) or not.

I often use exceptions in my test scripts for non-assertion purposes too.

1. Flag incomplete tests

   The problem with "TODO" comments is that you might forget them.

   ```
   it "next test" do
     # TODO
   end
   ```

   I like this way better.

   ```
   it "next test" do
     raise "TO BE DONE"
   end
   ```

2. Stop test execution during debugging a test

   Sometimes, you want to utilize automated tests to get you to a certain page in the application quickly.

   ```
   # test steps ...
   raise "Stop here, I take over from now. I delete this later."
   ```

   Ignorable test statement error When a test step can not be performed correctly, execution terminates and the test is marked as failed. However, failed to run certain test steps sometimes is OK. For example, we want to make sure a test starts with no active user session. If a user is currently signed in, try signing out; If a user has already signed out, performing signing out will fail. But it is acceptable.

   Here is an example to capture the error/failure in a test statement (in Ruby), and then ignore:

```
begin
  browser.link(text:  "Sign out").click
rescue => e
  # ignore
end
```

This seems quite complex. As usual, we can extract it into a reusable function:

```
# try operation, ignore if errors occur
def fail_safe(& block)
  begin
    yield
  rescue =>e
  end
end
```

Now You can do this in below one-line statement:

```
fail_safe{ browser.link(text:  "Sign out").click }
```

20.2 Read external file

We can use Ruby's built-in file i/o functions to read data, typically test data, from external files. Try to avoid referencing an external file using absolute path like below:

```
input_file = "C:\\temp\\in.xml" # Bad
content = File.read(input_file)
# ...
```

If the test scripts is copied to another machine, it might fail. A common practice is to put test data with the test scripts, and refer to them using relative path.

```
input_file = File.join(File.dirname(__FILE__), "testdata", "in.xml")
expect(File.exists?(input_file)).to be_truthy
content = File.read(input_file)
```

20.3 Data-Driven Tests with Excel

Data-Driven Testing means a test's input are driven from external sources, quite commonly in Excel or CSV files. For instance, if there is a list of user credentials with different roles and the login process is the same (but with different assertions), you can extract the test data from an excel spreadsheet and execute it one by one. Because Watir tests are in fact Ruby scripts, it is quite easy to do so.

A sample spreadsheet (*users.xls*) contains three username-password combination:

DESCRIPTION	LOGIN	PASSWORD	EXPECTED_TEXT
Valid Login	agileway	test	Login successful!
User name not exists	notexists	smartass	Login is not valid
Password not match	agileway	badpass	Password is not valid

The test scripts below reads the above and uses the login data to drive the browser to perform tests.

```
require 'spreadsheet'

browser = Watir::Browser.new
browser.goto("http://travel.agileway.net")

# Load Excel file
excel_file = File.join(File.dirname(__FILE__), "testdata", "users.xls")
excel_book = Spreadsheet.open excel_file
sheet1 = excel_book.worksheet(0) # first sheet

# Iterate each row in the first sheet
sheet1.each_with_index do |row, idx|
 next if idx == 0 # ignore first row
 desc, login, password, expected_text = row[0], row[1], row[2], row[3]
 browser.goto("http://travel.agileway.net")
 browser.text_field(name: "username").set login
 browser.text_field(name: "password").set password
 browser.button(value: "Sign in").click
 expect(browser.text).to include(expected_text)
 # if logged in OK, try log out, so next one can continue
 fail_safe{ browser.link(text:  "Sign off").click }
end
```

(The above test script requires spreadsheet *gem installed)*

20.4 Data-Driven Tests with CSV

A CSV (comma-separated values) file stores tabular data in plain-text form. CSV files are commonly used for importing into or exporting from applications. Comparing to Excel spreadsheets, a CSV file is a text file that contains only the pure data, not formatting.

Below is the CSV version of data driving test for the above user sign in example:

```
require 'csv'
csv_file = File.join(File.dirname(__FILE__), "testdata", "users.csv")
CSV.foreach(csv_file) do |row|
 # get user login details row by row
 login, password, expected_text = row[1], row[2], row[3]
 next if login == "LOGIN" # ignore first row
 browser.goto("http://travel.agileway.net")
 browser.text_field(name: "username").set login
 browser.text_field(name: "password").set password
 browser.button(value: "Sign in").click
 expect(browser.text).to include(expected_text)
 # if logged in OK, try log out, so next one can continue
 fail_safe{ browser.link(text:  "Sign off").click }
end
```

20.5 Identify element IDs with dynamically generated long prefixes

You can use regular expression to identify the static part of element ID or NAME. Below is a HTML fragment for a text box, we could tell some part of ID or NAME are machine generated (which might be different for next build), and the part "AppName" is meaningful.

```
<input id="ctl00_m_g_dcb0d043_e7f0_4128_99c6_71c113f45dd8_ctl00_tAppName_I"
  name="ctl00$m$g_dcb0d043_e7f0_4128_99c6_71c113f45dd8$ctl00$tAppName"/>
```

If we can later verify that 'AppName' is static for each text box, the test script below will work. Basically it instructs Watir to find ID element ends with "tApName_I".

```
browser.text_field(id: /tApName_I$/).set("I still can")
```

20.6 Sending special keys such as Enter to an element or browser

You can use .send_keys method to send special keys to a web control.

```
browser.text_field(id: "username").set("agileway")
sleep 1 # sleep for seeing the effect

# select all (Ctrl+A) then press backspace
browser.text_field(id: "username").send_keys([:control, 'a'], :backspace)
sleep 1
browser.text_field(id: "username").append("testwisely")
browser.text_field(id: "username").send_keys(:enter)
```

Some common special keys:

```
:backspace
:delete
:tab
:control
:shift
:alt
:page_up
:arrow_down
:home
:end
:escape
:enter
:meta
:command
```

The full list can be found at Selenium::WebDriver::Keys documentation[1].

---

[1]http://selenium.googlecode.com/svn/trunk/docs/api/rb/Selenium/WebDriver/Keys.html

20.7 Use of Unicode in test scripts

Watir does support Unicode. Test script files containing Unicode characters have to use UTF-8 encoding. This is easy to do, just insert `# encoding utf-8` at the beginning of test script files.

```
# encoding: UTF-8

# ...

browser.label(id: "unicode_test").text.should == "▨▨"
browser.text_field(id: "user").set("▨▨▨▨▨▨▨▨")
```

20.8 Extract a group of dynamic data : verify search results in order

The below is a sortable table, i.e., users can sort table columns in ascending or descending order by clicking the header.

Product	Released	URL
BuildWise	2010	https://testwisely.com/buildwise
ClinicWise	2013	https://clinicwise.net
SiteWise CMS	2014	http://sitewisecms.com
TestWise	2007	https://testwisely.com/testwise

To verify sorting, we need to extract all the data in the sorted column then verify the data in desired order. Knowledge of coding with List or Array is required.

```
browser.goto(site_url + "/data_grid.html")
sleep 0.5
browser.th(id: "heading_product").click  # first asc
first_cells = browser.tds(xpath: "//tbody/tr/td[1]")
product_names = first_cells.collect{|x| x.text}
expect(product_names).to eq(product_names.sort)

browser.th(id: "heading_product").click   # change sorting
sleep 0.5
first_cells = browser.tds(xpath: "//tbody/tr/td[1]")
product_names = first_cells.collect[|x| x.text}
expect(product_names).to eq(product_names.sort.reverse)
```

This approach is not limited to data in tables. The below script extracts the scores from the elements like `<span class='score'>98</span>`.

```
score_elems = driver.spans(xpath: "//div[@id='results']//span[@class='score']")
scores = score_elems.collect{|x| x.text.to_i }
# ...
```

20.9 Verify uniqueness of a set of data

Like the recipe above, extract data and store them in an array first, then compare the number of elements in the array with another one without duplicates.

```
second_cells = browser.tds(xpath: "//tbody/tr/td[2]")
years_released = second_cells.collect{|x| x.text}
expect(years_released.size).to eq(years_released.uniq.size)
```

20.10 Extract dynamic visible data rows from a results table

Many web search forms have filtering options that hide unwanted result entries.

☐ Test automation products only

Product	Released	URL	
ClinicWise	2013	https://clinicwise.net	Like
BuildWise	2010	https://testwisely.com/buildwise	Like
SiteWise CMS	2014	http://sitewisecms.com	Like
TestWise	2007	https://testwisely.com/testwise	Like

Displaying 1 - 4 of 4

The test scripts below verify the first product name and click the corresponding 'Like' button.

```
browser.goto(site_url + "/data_grid.html")
rows = browser.trs(xpath: "//table[@id='grid']/tbody/tr")
expect(rows.count).to eq(4)
first_product_name = browser.td(xpath: "//table[@id='grid']//tbody/tr[1]/td[1]").text
expect(first_product_name).to eq("ClinicWise")
browser.button(xpath: "//table[@id='grid']//tbody/tr[1]/td/button").click
```

Now check "Test automation products only" check box, and only two products are shown.

☑ Test automation products only

Product	Released	URL	
BuildWise	2010	https://testwisely.com/buildwise	Like
TestWise	2007	https://testwisely.com/testwise	Like

Displaying 1 - 4 of 4

```
browser.checkbox(id: "test_products_only_flag").click
sleep 0.2
# Error: Element is not currently visible
browser.button(xpath: "//table[@id='grid']//tbody/tr[1]/td/button").click
```

The last test statement would fail with an error "*Element is not currently visible*". After checking the "Test automation products only" check box, we see only 2 rows on screen. However, there are still 4 rows in the page, the other two are hidden.

```
▼ <tbody>
  ▶ <tr class="service_products" style="display: none;">…</tr> == $0
  ▶ <tr>…</tr>
  ▶ <tr class="service_products" style="display: none;">…</tr>
  ▶ <tr>…</tr>
  </tbody>
```

The button identified by this XPath `//table[@id='grid']//tbody/tr[1]/td/button` is now a hidden one, therefore unable to click.

A solution is to extract the visible rows to an array, then we could check them by index.

```
displayed_rows = browser.trs(xpath: "//table[@id='grid']//tbody/tr[not(contains(@style,'d\
isplay: none'))]")
expect(displayed_rows.count).to eq(2)
first_row_elem = displayed_rows[0]
new_first_product_name = first_row_elem.td(xpath: "td[1]").text
expect(new_first_product_name).to eq("BuildWise")
first_row_elem.button(xpath: "td/button").click
```

20.11 Extract dynamic text following a pattern using Regex

To use dynamic data created from the application, e.g. receipt number, we need to extract them out. Ideally, those data are marked by dedicated IDs such as `<span id='receipt_-number'></span>`. However, it is not always the case, i.e., the data are mixed with other text.

The most commonly used approach (in programming) is to extract data with Regular Expression. Regular Expression (abbreviated *regex* or *regexp*) is a pattern of characters that finds matching text. Almost every programming language supports regular expression, with minor differences.

The test script below will extract "V7H67U" and "2015-11-9" from the text Your coupon code: V7H67U used by 2015-11-9, and enter the extracted coupon code in the text box.

```
browser.goto(site_url + "/coupon.html")
browser.button(id: "get_coupon_btn").click
# Your coupon code: <b>H8ZVTA</b> used by <b>2015-11-9</b>
coupon_text = browser.element(id: "details").wait_until(&:present?).text
if coupon_text =~ /coupon code:\s+(\w+) used by\s([\d|-]+)/
  coupon_code = $1
  expiry_date = $2
  browser.text_field(name: "coupon").send_keys(coupon_code)
else
  raise "Error: no valid coupon returned"
end
```

Regular expression is very powerful and it does take some time to master it. To get it going for simple text matching, however, is not hard. Google 'ruby regular expression' shall return some good tutorials, and Rubular[2] is a helpful tool to let you try out regular expression online.

20.12 Quick extract pattern text in comments with Regex

The way shown in previous recipe is how typical regular expression is used in coding. Ruby's String[3] has built-in support for Regex to extract pattern text in a simpler way. For example, to extract the hidden version number (in comments) on a web page like below.

```
<!-- Version: 2.19.1.9798 -->
```

Just needs one line statement.

```
(driver.page_source)[/<!-- Version: (.*?) -->/, 1]
```

The (.?) is to match the text between <!-- and -->, and 1 is to return the first capturing group. If there is no match, nil is returned.

Here is a complete version of test script to verify the version number.

---

[2]http://rubular.com/
[3]http://ruby-doc.org/core-2.2.0/String.html#method-i-5B-5D

```
browser.goto(site_url + "/index.html")
ver = (browser.html)[/<!-- Version: (.*?) -->/, 1]
puts ver # in format of 2.19.1.9798
expect(ver.split(".").length).to eq(4)
expect(ver.split(".")[0]).to eq("2")    # major version
expect(ver.split(".")[1]).to eq("19")   # minor version
```

How about extracting multiple occurrences of a pattern text in a web page?

```
<!-- TestWise Version: 4.7.1 -->
...
<!-- ClinicWise Version: 3.0.6 -->
```

Use String's scan method, which returns an array of matched text for a given pattern in Regex.

```
app_vers = browser.html.scan(/<!-- (\w+) Version: (.*?) -->/)
puts app_vers.inspect
expect(app_vers.size).to eq(2)
expect(app_vers.last).to eq(["ClinicWise", "3.0.6"])
```

20.13 Invoke element's JavaScript events such as 'onclick'

In the example below, when user clicks on the text field, the tip text ('*Max 20 characters*') is shown.

Example page

Max 20 characters

HTML Source

```
<input type="text" name="person_name" onclick="$('#tip').show();"
  onchange="change_person_name(this.value);"/>
<span id="tip" style="display:none; margin-left: 20px; color:gray;">Max 20 characters
  </span>
```

When we use normal `text_field.set` in Watir, it enters the text OK, but the tip text is not displayed.

```
browser.text_field(name: "person_name").set "Test Wise"
```

We can add `fire_event('onclick')` to achieve it.

```
browser.text_field(name: "person_name").set "Wise Tester"
expect(browser.span(id: "tip").present?).to be_falsey
browser.text_field(name: "person_name").fire_event("onclick")
expect(browser.span(id: "tip").present?).to be_truthy
```

Watir-Classic: Simulate typing in a text field?

For pages with JavaScript monitoring keystrokes in a text field, you can set Watir in 'typing' mode.

```
elem = browser.text_field(id: "username")
elem.requires_typing
elem.append("Test")
sleep 1
elem.append("Wise")
```

21. Optimization

Working test scripts is just the first test step to successful test automation. As automated tests are executed often, and we all know the application changes frequently too. Therefore, it is important that we need our test scripts to be

- Fast
- Easy to read
- Concise

In this chapter, I will show some examples to optimize test scripts.

21.1 Assert text in page_source is faster than the text

To verify a piece of text on a web page, frequently for assertion, we can use `browser.html` or `browser.text`. Besides the obvious different output, there are big performance differences too. To get a text view (for a whole page or a web control), WebDriver needs to analyse the raw HTML to generate the text view, and it takes time. We usually do not notice that time when the raw HTML is small. However, for a large web page like the WebDriver standard[1] (over 430KB in file size), incorrect use of 'text view' will slow your test execution significantly.

---

[1]http://www.w3.org/TR/webdriver/

```
browser.goto(site_url + "/WebDriverStandard.html")
start_time = Time.now
expect(browser.text).to include("language-neutral wire protocol")
puts("Method 1: Search whole document text took #{Time.now - start_time} seconds")

start_time = Time.now
expect(browser.html).to include("language-neutral wire protocol")
puts("Method 2: Search whole document HTML took #{Time.now - start_time} seconds")
```

Let's see the difference.

```
Method 1: Search page text took 1.632 seconds
Method 2: Search page HTML took 0.07 seconds
```

21.2 Getting text from more specific element is faster

A rule of thumb is that we save execution time by narrowing down a more specific control. The two assertion statements largely achieve the same purpose but with big difference in execution time.

```
expect(browser.text).to include("language-neutral wire protocol")
```

Execution time: **1.66** seconds

```
expect(browser.section(id: "abstract").text).to include("language-neutral wire protocol")
```

Execution time: **0.1** seconds

21.3 Avoid programming if-else block code if possible

It is common that programmers write test scripts in a similar way as coding applications, while I cannot say it is wrong. For me, I prefer simple, concise and easy to read test scripts.

1. Reduce three line test statements to one by putting `if` or `unless` after the test statement

```
if $verbose_mode
  puts "Page Title => #{driver.title}"
end
```

change to

```
puts driver.title if $verbose_mode
```

2. Replace if-else with ternary operator ? :

```
ticket_number = browser.label(id: "ticket_no").text
if reference_number =~ /^VIP/     # special guest
  expect(browser.label(id: "special_notes").text).to eq("Please go upstairs")
else
  expect(browser.label(id: "special_notes").text).to eq("")
end
```

change to

```
expect(browser.label(id: "special_notes").text).to eq(
  reference_number =~ /^VIP/ ? "Please go upstairs" : "")
```

21.4 Use variable to cache not-changed data

Commonly, I saw people wrote tests like the below to check multiple texts on a page.

```
browser.goto(site_url + "/WebDriverStandard.html")
expect(browser.text).to include("Firefox")
expect(browser.text).to include("chrome")
expect(browser.text).to include("W3C")
```

Execution time: **5.18** seconds

The above three test statements are very inefficient, as every test statement calls `browser.text`, this can be a quite expensive operation when a web page is large.

Solution: use a variable to store the text (view) of the web page, a very common practice in programming.

```
the_page_text = browser.text
expect(the_page_text).to include("Firefox")
expect(the_page_text).to include("chrome")
expect(the_page_text).to include("W3C")
```

Execution time: **1.50** seconds

As you can see, we get quite constant execution time no matter how many assertions we perform on that page, as long as the page text we are checking is not changing.

21.5 Enter large text into a text box

We commonly use send_keys to enter text into a text box. When the text string you want to enter is quite large, e.g. thousands of characters, try to avoid using send_keys, as it is not efficient. Here is an example.

```
long_str = "START" + '0' * 1024 * 5  + "END" # just over 5K
browser.textarea(id: "comments").set(long_str)
```

Execution time: **3.39** seconds.

When this test is executed in Chrome, you can see a batch of text 'typed' into the text box. Furthermore, there might be a limited number of characters that WebDriver 'send' into a text box for browsers at one time. I have seen test scripts that broke long text into trunks and then sent them one by one, not elegant.

The **solution** is actually quite simple: using JavaScript.

```
browser.execute_script("document.getElementById('comments').value = arguments[0];", long_\
str)
```

Execution time: **0.01** seconds

21.6 Use Environment Variables to change test behaviours dynamically

Typically, there are more than one test environment we need to run automated tests against, and we might want to run the same test in different browsers now and then. I saw the test scripts like the below often in projects.

```
$SITE_URL = "https://physio.clinicwise.net"
# $SITE_URL = "http://demo.poolwise.net"
$TARGET_BROWSER = "chrome"
# $TARGET_BROWSER = "firefox"
driver = Selenium::WebDriver.for($TARGET_BROWSER.to_sym)
driver.navigate.to($SITE_URL)
```

It works like this: testers comment and uncomment a set of test statements to let test script run against different servers in different browsers. This is not an ideal approach, because it is inefficient, error prone and introducing unnecessary check-ins (changing test script files with no changes to testing logic).

A simple solution is to use agreed environment variables, so that the target server URL and browser type can be set externally, outside the test scripts.

```
# if not defined, will use default values after 'rescue'
$SITE_URL = ENV["BASE_URL"].to_s rescue "https://physio.clinicwise.net"
$TARGET_BROWSER = ENV["TARGET_BROWSER"].to_sym rescue :firefox
# ...
driver = Selenium::WebDriver.for($TARGET_BROWSER)
driver.navigate.to($SITE_URL)
```

For example, to run this test against another server in Chrome, run below commands.

```
> set TARGET_BROWSER=chrome
> set SITE_URL=http://yake.clinicwise.net
> rspec login_spec.rb
```

This approach is commonly used in Continuous Testing process.

21.7 Test web site in two languages

The test scripts below to test user authentication for two test sites, the same application in two languages: *http://physio.clinicwise.net* in English and *http://yake.clinicwise.net* in Chinese. While the business features are the same, the text shown on two sites are different, so are the test user accounts.

```
$SITE_URL = ENV["SITE_URL"] rescue "http://physio.clinicwise.net"
browser = Watir::Browser.new
browser.goto($SITE_URL)

if $TARGET_SITE_URL =~ /physio/
  browser.text_field(id: "username").set("natalie")
  browser.text_field(id: "password").set("test")
  browser.button(id: "signin_button").click
  expect(browser.html).to include("Signed in successfully.")
elsif $TARGET_SITE_URL =~ /yake/
  browser.text_field(id: "username").set("tuo")
  browser.text_field(id: "password").set("test")
  browser.button(id: "signin_button").click
  expect(browser.text).to include("▨▨▨▨")
end
```

Though the above test scripts work, it seems lengthy and repetitive.

```
def is_cn?
  $SITE_URL =~ /yake/
end
```

```
it "Test user authentication in both English and Chinese"
  browser.text_field(id: "username").set(is_cn? ? "tuo" : "natalie")
  browser.text_field(id: "password").set("test")
  browser.button(id: "signin_button").click
  expect(browser.text).to include(is_cn? ? "▨▨▨▨": "Signed in successfully.")
end
```

Using IDs can greatly save multi-language testing

When doing multi-language testing, try not to use the actual text on the page for non user-entering operations. For example, the test statements are not optimal.

```
browser.link(:text, "Register").click
# or below with some programming logic ...
browser.link(:text, "Registre").click   # french
browser.link(:text, "▨▨").click         # chinese
```

Using IDs is much simpler.

```
browser.link(id: "register_link").click
```

This works for all languages.

21.8 Multi-language testing with lookups

We can extend the approach used in previous recipe (`if-elsif-elsif-else`) to work with multiple languages.

```
# return the current language used on the site
def site_lang
  # ...
end

# in test case
if site_lang == "chinese"
  browser.text_field(id: "username").send_keys("wang")
elsif site_lang == "french"
  browser.text_field(id: "username").send_keys("dupont")
else # default to english
  browser.text_field(id: "username").send_keys("natalie")
end

browser.text_field(id: "password").send_keys("test")
browser.button(id: "signin_button").click
```

If this is going to be used only once, the above is fine. However, these login test steps will be used heavily, which will lead to lengthy and hard to maintain test scripts.

Solution: centralize the logic with lookups.

```
def user_lookup(username)
  case site_lang
  when "chinese"
    "hongyu"
  when "french"
    "dupont"
  else
    "natalie"
  end
end

# in test case
browser.text_field(id: "username").set(user_lookup("natalie"))
browser.text_field(id: "password").set("test")
browser.button(id: "signin_button").click
```

Astute readers may point out, "You over-simplify the cases, there surely will be more test users." Yes, that's true. I was trying to the simplest way to convey the lookup. Here is a more complete solution.

```
user_lang_lookups = {
  "natalie" => {"english"=>"natalie", "chinese"=>"hongyu", "french"=>"dupont"},
  "mark" => {"english"=>"mark", "chinese"=>"li", "french"=>"marc"},
  # ...
}
browser.text_field(id: "username").set(user_lang_lookups["natalie"][site_lang()])
browser.text_field(id: "password").set("test")
browser.button(id: "signin_button").click
```

In summary, the test user in a chosen language (English in above example) is used as the key to look up for other languages. The equivalent user of "natalie" in French is "dupont".

Some, typically programmers, write the test scripts like the below.

```
def get_admin_user
  # logic goes here
end

browser.text_field(id: "username").set(get_admin_user())
```

If there are only a handful users, it may be OK. But I often see hard-to-read test statements such as get_register_user_1() and get_manager_2(). I cannot say this approach is wrong, I just prefer using 'personas'. But I am against reading test users from external configuration files, which generally I found, hard to maintain.

22. Gotchas

Writing test scripts in Watir is much more than knowing the API, it involves programming, HTML, JavaScript and web browsers. There are cases that can be confusing to newcomers.

22.1 Test starts browser but no execution with blank screen

A very possible cause is that the version of installed WebDriver is not compatible with the version of your browser. Here is a screenshot of Firefox 41.0.2 started by a Selenium WebDriver 2.44.0 test (*Watir depends on Selenium-WebDriver*).

The test hung there. After I upgraded Selenium WebDriver to 2.45, the test ran fine.

This can happen to Chrome too. With both browsers and Selenium WebDriver get updated quite frequently, in a matter of months, it is not that surprising to get the incompatibility issues. For test engineers who are not aware of this, it can be quite confusing as the tests might be running fine the day before and no changes have been made since.

Once knowing the cause, the solutions are easy:

- Upgrade both Selenium WebDriver and browsers to the latest version

Browsers such as Chrome usually turn on auto-upgrade by default, I suggest upgrading to the latest Selenium WebDriver several days after it is released.

- Lock Selenium WebDriver and browsers.

Turn off auto-upgrade in browser and be thoughtful on upgrading Selenium WebDriver.

 ## Be aware of browser and driver changes

One day I found over 40 test failures (out of about 400) by surprise on the latest continuous testing build. There were little changes since the last build, in which all tests passed. I quickly figured out the cause: Chrome auto-upgraded to v44. Chrome 44 with the ChromeDriver 2.17 changed the behaviour of clicking hyperlinks. After clicking a link, sometimes test executions immediately continue to the next operation without waiting for the "clicking link" operation to finish.

```
driver.find_element(id: "new_client").click
sleep 0.5 # hack for chrome v44, make sure the link is clicked
```

A week later, I noticed the only line in the change log of ChromeDriver v2.18:

```
"Changes include many bug fixes that allow ChromeDriver to work more reliably with Chrome\
    44+."
```

22.2 Failed to assert copied text in browser

To answer this, let's start with an example. What we see in a browser (Internet Explorer)

BOLD *Italic*

```
Text assertion
(new line before)!
```

is the result of rendering the page source (HTML) below in Internet Explorer:

```
<p id="text"> <b>BOLD</b>   <i>Italic</i></p>

<pre id="formatted">Text assertion  
(new line before)!</pre>
```

As you can see, there are differences. Test scripts can be written to check the text view (what we saw) on browsers or its raw page source (HTML). To complicate things a little more, old versions of browsers may return slightly different results.

Do not worry. As long as you understand that the text shown in browsers are coming from raw HTML source, and after a few attempts, this is usually not a problem. Here are the test scripts for checking text and source for above example:

```
# tags in source not in text
expect(browser.text).to include("BOLD Italic")
expect(browser.html).to include("<b>BOLD</b>  <i>Italic</i>")

# HTML entities in source but shown as space in text
expect(browser.text).to include("assertion  \r\n(new line before)")

# note the second character after assertion is non-breakable space ( )
expect(browser.html).to include("assertion  \n(new line before)")
```

22.3 The same test works for Chrome, but not IE

Chrome, Firefox and IE are different products and web browsers are very complex software. Comparing to other testing frameworks, Selenium WebDriver provides better support for all major browsers. Still there will be some operations work differently on one than another.

```
if  browser.driver.browser == :firefox
  # firefox specific test statement
elsif browser.driver.browser.to_s ==  "chrome"
  # chrome specific test statement
else
  raise "unsupported browser: #{browser.driver.browser}"
end
```

Some might say that it will require a lot of work. Yes, cross-browser testing is associated with more testing effort, obviously. However, from my observation, few IT managers acknowledge this. That's why cross-testing is talked a lot, but rarely gets done.

22.4 Element is not clickable or not visible

Some controls such as textfields, even when they are not visible in the current browser window, WebDriver will move the focus to them. Some other controls such as buttons, may be not. In that case, though the element is found, it is not clickable.

The solution is to make the target control visible in browser.

1. Scroll the window to make the control visible

   Find out the control's position and scroll to it.

   ```
   elem = browser.button(name: "submit_action_2")
   elem_pos = elem.location.y
   driver.execute_script("window.scroll(0, #{elem_pos})")
   ```

   Or scroll to the top / bottom of page.

   ```
   browser.execute_script("window.scrollTo(0, document.body.scrollHeight);")
   ```

2. A hack, call send_keys to a text field nearby, if there is one.

22.5 Lack knowledge of the programming language

Unfamiliar to the programming language used for Watir tests can cause confusion too. For example, one tester came to me saying that his test scripts (shown below) was hanging for no apparent reasons.

```
sleep{1}
```

It turned out that it was a typo, resulting into a valid ruby code to execute a block (which sleeps indefinitely). He meant sleep(1).

23. Watir with Cucumber

Most of tests in this book are written in RSpec syntax, as explained in Chapter 1. There is another popular BDD framework: Cucumber[1]. You can find plenty of Cucumber tutorials on Internet. Here I will just provide a sample test project (available on the book site) that you can run some cucumber tests right away.

Firstly, download the recipe tests from the site if you haven't done so. This is how it looks like in TestWise.

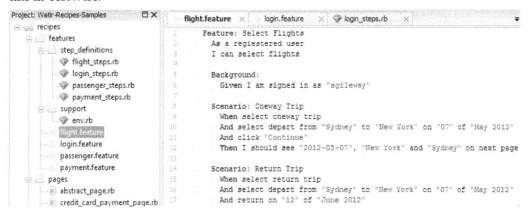

As you can see, there are more stuff than RSpec. There are four kind of files:

- Features, e.g. *login.feature*. The top level test script file.
- Step definitions, e.g. *step_definitions/login_steps.rb*. This contains definitions (actual test steps driving the browser) for the steps in the features.
- Support files, e.g. *support/env.rb*. Usually just the one env.rb, which sets up Cucumber's execution environment.
- Page classes, e.g. *pages/flight_page.rb* . This is optional, but a common practice to make writing and maintaining test easier. If you decide to write tests in RSpec and Cucumber, these page classes are reusable.

---

[1]http://cukes.info/

23.1 How Watir is integrated with Cucumber?

The '*support/env.rb*' is the key file. The code fragment below in *env.rb* does four things:

- load *watir* gem
- load page classes
- initialize a watir browser instance
- make the browser instance (@browser) available to step definitions via *Before* hook

```
require 'watir'
require 'test/unit/assertions'

# Load page classes
require File.join(File.dirname(__FILE__), "../../pages/abstract_page.rb")
Dir["#{File.dirname(__FILE__)}/../../pages/*_page.rb"].each {
  |file| load file }

$BASE_URL = "http://travel.agileway.net"

browser =  Watir::Browser.new(the_browser)
World(Test::Unit::Assertions)

Before do
  @browser = browser
  # @browser.goto(...)
end
```

The Before hook is called before executing each scenario.

In step definitions (*_steps.rb*), we can directly use @browser.

```
Given /^I am on the home page$/ do
  @browser.goto("http://travel.agileway.net")
end
```

I would suggest using page objects in step definitions, which will make test maintenance a lot easier.

```
When /^I enter "(.*?)" and "(.*?)" as passenger name$/ do |fname, lname|
  sleep 1
  @passenger_page = PassengerPage.new(@browser)
  @passenger_page.enter_first_name(fname)
  @passenger_page.enter_last_name(lname)
end
```

23.2 Execute Cucumber tests

From Command Line

As long as you have *cucumber* gem installed, you can run cucumber tests from command line.

```
cucumber features/login.feature
```

Here is a sample output:

```
Feature: User Authentication
  As a registered user
  I can log in

  Scenario: User can log in successfully  # features/login.feature:5
  Given I am on the home page    # features/step_definitions/login_steps.rb:9
  When enter user name "agileway" and password "testwise" # features/step_definitions/log\
in_steps.rb:13
  And click "Sign in" button    # features/step_definitions/login_steps.rb:18
  Then I am logged in           # features/step_definitions/login_steps.rb:22

1 scenario (1 passed)
4 steps (4 passed)
0m4.128s
```

Please be aware, cucumber execution can be a bit restrictive. You may assume the command below shall work:

```
cd features
cucumber login.feature
```

But it doesn't: reporting step definitions were not found.

```
1 scenario (1 undefined)
4 steps (4 undefined)
```

Work with Cucumber in IDE

Obviously it depends on what tool you use. TestWise supports both RSpec and Cucumber, the way to execute tests are the same.

Besides executions, I found two useful features when working with Cucumber in IDE (taking TestWise as an example below):

- Generate step definition skeleton

  After writing the scenario, manually construct step definitions is difficult (requires regular expression knowledge). In TestWise, just right click the feature file to generate:

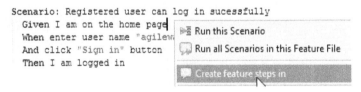

Then enter the file name for the step file. TestWise will create this file with shown skeleton in the right location (under step_definitions)

- Navigate to step definition file from a scenario step

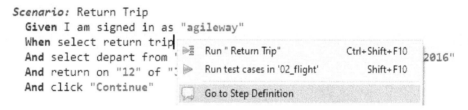

I think all tools 'support Cucumber' should have these functions.

23.3 Cucumber or RSpec?

My short answer is: RSpec (with page classes) then Cucumber if Cucumber is a must.

Quite often, the choice of Cucumber is dictated by a manager who has little understanding of test automation. In this case, the benefits of Cucumber may not be realized but the team is hit with extra maintenance efforts. I have already covered this topic in my other book Practical Web Test Automation[2].

---

[2]https://leanpub.com/practical-web-test-automation

Afterword

First of all, if you haven't downloaded the recipe test scripts from the book site, I strongly recommend you to do so. It is free for readers who have purchased the ebook through Leanpub.

This book comes with two formats: *Ebook* and *Paper book*. I originally thought there won't be much demand for printed book, as the convenient 'search ability' of ebooks is good for this kind of solution books. However, during on-site consultation, I found some testers I worked with kept borrowing my printed proof-copy and wanted to buy it. It's why I released the paper book on Amazon as well.

Practice makes perfect

Like any other skills, you will get better at it by practising more.

- **Write tests**

  Many testers would like to practise test automation with Watir/Selenium WebDriver, but they don't have a good target application to write tests against. Here I make one of my applications available for you: WhenWise sandbox site[3]. WhenWise is a modern web application using popular web technologies such as AJAX and Material Design. I have written 500 Selenium WebDriver tests for WhenWise. Execution of all tests takes more than 5 hours on a single machine. If you like, you can certainly practise writing tests against WhenWise sandbox server.

  WhenWise is also a show case of web applications designed (based on the popular Material Design) for testing, which means it is easier to write automated tests against it. Our every Selenium test starts with calling a database reset: visit *https://whenwise.agileway.net/reset*, which will reset the database to a seeded state.

Database reset OK. Current access token expires in 22 minutes

---

[3]https://whenwise.agileway.net

- **Improve programming skills**

  It requires programming skills to effectively use Selenium WebDriver. For readers with no programming background, the good news is that the programming knowledge required for writing test scripts is much less comparing to coding applications, as you have seen in this book. If you like learning with hands-on practices, check out Learn Ruby Programming by Examples[4].

Successful Test Automation

I believe that you are well equipped to cope with most testing scenarios if you have mastered the recipes in this book. However, this only applies to your ability to write individual tests. Successful test automation also requires developing and maintaining many automated test cases while software applications change frequently.

- **Maintain test scripts to keep up with application changes**

  Let's say you have 100 automated tests that all pass. The changes developers made in the next build will affect some of your tests. As this happens too often, many automated tests will fail. The only way to keep the test script maintainable is to adopt good test design practices (such as reusable functions and page objects) and efficient refactoring. Check out my other book *Practical Web Test Automation*[5].

- **Shorten test execution time to get quick feedback**

  With growing number of test cases, so is the test execution time. This leads to a long feedback gap from the time programmers committed the code to the time test execution completes. If programmers continue to develop new features/fixes during the gap time, it can easily get into a tail-chasing problem. This will hurt the team's productivity badly. Executing automated tests in a Continuous Testing server with various techniques (such as distributing test to run in parallel) can greatly shorten the feedback time. Check out my other book *Practical Continuous Testing*[6].

Best wishes for your test automation!

---

[4]https://leanpub.com/learn-ruby-programming-by-examples-en
[5]https://leanpub.com/practical-web-test-automation
[6]https://leanpub.com/practical-continuous-testing

Resources

Recipe test scripts

http://zhimin.com/books/bought-watir-recipes[7]

Username: `agileway`
Password: `STORYWISE11`

Log in with the above, or scan QR Code to access directly.

Books

- **Practical Web Test Automation**[8] by Zhimin Zhan

  Solving individual Watir challenges (what this book is for) is far from achieving test automation success. *Practical Web Test Automation* is the book to guide you to the test automation success, topics include:
  - Maintainable Test Design
  - Page object model
  - Functional Testing Refactorings
  - Cross-browser testing against IE, Firefox and Chrome
  - Strategies on team collaboration and test automation adoption in projects and organizations
- **Practical Continuous Testing**[9] by Zhimin Zhan

  Continuous Testing (CT) is the key process of DevOps. This books guides you to manage executing your Watir tests in a CT server.
- **Selenium WebDriver Recipes in Ruby**[10] by Zhimin Zhan

  Selenium-WebDriver is the most widely used testing library for web applications. While we can use Watir-WebDriver (with Selenium-WebDriver underneath), being able to write Selenium-WebDriver tests is still a necessary skill for a web automation tester.
- **Learn Ruby Programming by Examples**[11] by Zhimin Zhan and Courtney Zhan

---

[7]http://zhimin.com/books/bought-watir-recipes
[8]https://leanpub.com/practical-web-test-automation
[9]https://leanpub.com/practical-continuous-testing
[10]https://leanpub.com/selenium-recipes-in-ruby
[11]https://leanpub.com/learn-ruby-programming-by-examples-en

Master Ruby programming to empower you to write test scripts.

- **API Testing Recipes in Ruby**[12] by Zhimin Zhan

The problem-solving guide to testing APIs such as SOAP and REST web services in Ruby language.

Websites

- **HTML Elements supported by Watir** (https://github.com/watir/watir/wiki/HTML-Elements-Supported-by-Watir[13])
- **Watir Home** (http://watir.com[14])
- **RSpec** (http://rspec.info[15])
- **Cucumber** (http://cukes.info[16])
- **TestWisely blog**[17] by Zhimin

Tools

- **TestWise IDE** (http://testwisely.com/testwise[18])

AgileWay's next generation functional testing IDE supporting Selenium, Watir with RSpec and Cucumber. TestWise Community Edition is free.

- **BuildWise** (http://testwisely.com/buildwise[19])

AgileWay's free and open-source continuous build server, purposely designed for running automated UI tests with quick feedback.

- **Ruby Installer for Windows** (http://rubyinstaller.org/[20])

The standard Ruby Windows installer.

---

[12]https://leanpub.com/api-testing-recipes-in-ruby
[13]https://github.com/watir/watir/wiki/HTML-Elements-Supported-by-Watir
[14]http://watir.com
[15]http://rspec.info
[16]http://cukes.info
[17]https://zhiminzhan.medium.com
[18]http://testwisely.com/testwise
[19]http://testwisely.com/buildwise
[20]http://rubyinstaller.org/